Endorsements for
The Invisible Church:
Learning from the experiences of churchless Christians

If we are to build Christian communities that are genuinely mission-shaped and that shape a new future for the church, then the importance of listening to voices of people outside the church, especially those who have left, cannot be underestimated. This is an excellent book to facilitate that.

Phil Potter, Archbishops' Missioner and Fresh Expressions Team Leader

When a serious researcher like Steve Aisthorpe writes about churchless Christians instead of just writing them off, missional leaders need to be giving him their full attention.

David Walker, Bishop of Manchester

Here is a book dealing with one of the most significant issues of our time. While undergirded by rigorous academic research, it is eminently accessible and will be of deep interest to all who are interested in the changing nature of society, as well as the changing face of the church. In every chapter it aims to secure the reader's practical engagement. At once hopeful and challenging, this is a major contribution to reflection on the place of the church in contemporary society. I wish it a wide readership.

Angus Morrison, Moderator of the
General Assembly of the Church of Scotland

Great to hear the voices of people outside the church, especially those who have left!

Michael Moynagh, Director of Network Development and Consultant on
Theology and Practice with Fresh Expressions; Executive Theologian and
Researcher with the Centre for Pioneer Learning, Cambridge; author of
Being Church, Doing Life *and* Church for Every Context

I continue to meet the very people this book talks about, but the wider church is unsure how to react, because admitting this reality of churchless Christians poses deep questions about how church operates at present. The book is utterly honest about the problems we face but contributes realistically and constructively to the great re-imagination of the church – or ecclesial earthquake – that is going on in our day.

George Lings, Director, Church Army's Research Unit

Steve has turned his excellent research into a very accessible book that challenges us in the church as to how we respond to the many who have not rejected Christian faith, but have sort of rejected the church. Vitally, we are offered ways in which to respond to this challenge.

Stephen Skuce, Director of Scholarship, Research
and Innovation for the British Methodist Church

Steve Aisthorpe sheds invaluable light on a neglected but numerous group, those who have a Christian faith but do not attend a congregation. Steve's work is well researched, takes theology seriously and is pastorally wise. All church leaders can learn much from reading it.

David Goodhew, Director of Ministerial Practice, Durham University

I have said for a long time that the 'middle ground' is the most interesting place to look in terms of the religious life of this country. Steve Aisthorpe's empirically driven work enhances our understanding of this fascinating and constantly evolving field.

Grace Davie, Professor of Sociology, University of Exeter; author of
Religion in Britain: A persistent paradox

All involved in church leadership – indeed all exercised Christians – need to grapple with the issues at the heart of this highly readable book about the growing phenomenon of churchless Christians. What are they? How did they become such? And why? Steve Aisthorpe explores these questions, exploding en route a number of the facile explanations for the phenomenon. Despite the significant challenges raised by his research, Steve closes his book on a note of hope.

Hector Morrison, Principal, Highland Theological College,
University of the Highlands and Islands

Steve Aisthorpe makes a very valuable contribution to our understanding of the growing number of Christians who are active in mission but not part of local congregations. His insights, drawn from extensive and rigorous research, make us think afresh about what God is doing in the western, developed world. These insights are honed and shaped by reflections on Bible passages. Some of our traditional ways of thinking are challenged, so read with a mind open to what the Spirit is saying!

Elaine Duncan, Chief Executive, Scottish Bible Society

Steve Aisthorpe offers an original, insightful and authoritative voice on making visible and audible the invisible church of churchless Christians. His insights need to be taken seriously to understand God's presence and activity in today's world.

Leslie J. Francis, Professor of Religions and Education,
University of Warwick

The 'Invisible Church' is insightful, well researched and prophetic. If you're concerned about the future of the church in the West this is a must read. Through rigorous personal research and careful analysis, Steve Aisthorpe sketches the future of the church through the eyes of church-leavers.

Alan Jamieson, author of A Churchless Faith

The Invisible Church

Learning from the experiences
of churchless Christians

Steve Aisthorpe

SAINT ANDREW PRESS
Edinburgh

First published in 2016 by
SAINT ANDREW PRESS
121 George Street
Edinburgh EH2 4YN

Third impression October 2016

ISBN 978-0-86153-916-1

British Library Cataloguing in Publication Data
A catalogue record for this book is available from the British Library.

It is the publisher's policy to only use papers that are natural and
recyclable and that have been manufactured from timber grown in
renewable, properly managed forests. All of the manufacturing processes
of the papers are expected to conform to the environmental regulations of
the country of origin.

Typeset by Manila Typesetting

Printed and bound in the United Kingdom by
CPI Group (UK) Ltd

Contents

Acknowledgements

My journey towards a better understanding of the changes occurring in the Christian community has been a long one, but I have not travelled alone. I am particularly grateful to Professor Leslie Francis for his invaluable support and advice while undertaking the initial research. Sheila Reeves is owed a special debt of gratitude for her painstaking and uncomplaining labours in turning recorded interviews into accurate transcripts and turning the first drafts of this book into 'proper English'.

I know that some of you (most of you perhaps? What! All of you?) bought this book because of Dave Walker's pithy and thought-provoking cartoons. So thank you Dave for your valued contribution. When it's one of Dave's cartoons, a picture really does say a thousand words.

Special thanks are also due to John, Jon, Hilary, Lesley, Benjamin, Andrew, David, Grace and Stephen. Without their comments, questions, suggestions, encouragement and critique, this book would be less than it is. Staff and Council members of the Mission and Discipleship Council of the Church of Scotland have not only allowed me the time to pursue this research, but have been enthusiastic and supportive throughout, as has Ann Crawford and colleagues at Saint Andrew Press / Hymns Ancient and Modern.

Finally, and foremost, love and thanks to Liz, John and Scott for putting up with me banging on about this book for ages and tolerating my periods of 'writing lockdown'.

Bible quotations

Unless otherwise indicated, all scripture quotations are taken from the Holy Bible, New Living Translation, copyright © 1996, 2004, 2007, 2013 by Tyndale House Foundation. Used by permission of Tyndale House Publishers, Inc., Carol Stream, Illinois 60188. All rights reserved.

Other sources are:

ICB   International Children's Bible®, copyright © 1986, 1988, 1999, 2015 by Tommy Nelson. Used by permission.

KJV   King James Version.

MSG   The Message, E. H. Peterson, 1993 – 2002, Carol Stream, IL: NavPress.

NRSV   New Revised Standard Version Bible, Anglicized version, copyright © 1989 the Division of Christian Education of the National Council of the Churches of Christ in the United States of America. Used by permission. All rights reserved.

Phillips The New Testament in Modern English by J. B. Phillips, copyright © 1960, 1972 J. B. Phillips. Administered by The Archbishops' Council of the Church of England. Used by Permission.

RSV   Revised Standard Version of the Bible, copyright © 1946, 1952, and 1971 the Division of Christian Education of the National Council of the Churches of Christ in the United States of America. Used by permission. All rights reserved.

Introduction

Read This First!

Are you concerned for the health of the Church . . . discouraged by the decline of many congregations . . . a Christian, but not a church-goer? If your answer is 'yes' to any of these questions, then this book is for you.

We live in an era of unprecedented change. Indeed, history may well show that we lived through not just an era of change, but a change of era. At such a time as this, *The Invisible Church: Learning from the experiences of churchless Christians*, offers a trustworthy guide to the world behind the statistics of apparent decline. In the stories of people who have shared their experiences of faith and church, a wealth of encouragement, wisdom and inspiration is unearthed.

Here is a resource that is both readable and reliable. It is rooted in rigorous empirical evidence, but also practical. Extensive research among people who are Christians, but not church-goers, is explained with clarity. *The Invisible Church* is not a comprehensive presentation of research finding, but readers are signposted to places where the detailed data underlying the book is freely available online. Each chapter explores a key aspect of the monumental changes that are occurring in the Christian community across the Western world. After reflecting on a relevant Bible passage, we hear the voices of Christians who are not church-goers as they recount their experiences; we consider their perspectives as we review the findings of extensive surveys. Having been centred in scripture and reminded of the evidence, we then explore some of the processes at work behind the decline of traditional church-going and the rise of 'churchless faith' and ask ourselves what all of this might mean for our own situation.

The opening chapters (1–3) explore the 'what?' of 'churchless faith'. The changing shape of the worldwide Christian community is explained. Then, in Chapter 4, the 'how?' of church-leaving is examined. Chapters 5 to 9 investigate the 'why?' questions. Why have those who have been part of local churches for many years left the congregation? Why have some of those who have embraced the Christian faith through participating in courses such as Alpha, Christianity Explored, etc., not then engaged with a local church? Finally, Chapter 10 considers the future of the Church, given current trends.

The Church's current trajectory is sometimes depicted as a nose-dive, but the reader is encouraged to move beyond simplistic assumptions based on the statistics of where people spend Sunday morning and to recognise that a growing body of evidence paints a picture which is less about decline and more about transition. The Church is changing and the future is hope-filled.

CHAPTER I

Forgotten but not gone

In this chapter, we follow Jesus' call to 'open our eyes' and see what is going on right under our noses. Churchless faith is a feature of the dramatic and momentous change going on in Western society. Here, new research provides a window into the world behind the statistics of so-called decline and enables us to understand what is really going on – why this is an exciting time and why declining church attendance may not be all that it seems.

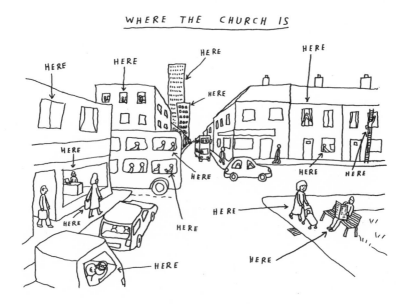

I

Jesus said . . . As you look around right now, wouldn't
you say that in about four months it will be time
to harvest? Well, I'm telling you to open your eyes
and take a good look at what's right in front of you.
These Samaritan fields are ripe. It's harvest time!

John 4:34–35 (MSG)

Open your eyes

The Palestinian countryside is challenging terrain from an agricul-
tural point of view. The soil is rocky. The ground is parched for
much of the year. Cultivation is a battle requiring both toil and
tenacity. So, the sight of a sea of golden corn waving in the breeze,
'ripe and ready to be harvested', was unusual. However, Jesus and
his disciples were close to Sychar in Samaria (John 4:5), a region
of unusual fertility, renowned for its abundant harvests.[1]

The thought of travelling through Samaria would have been
abhorrent to the disciples. The feud between Jews and Samaritans
had been festering for centuries. Racial rivalry, religious dispute
and ethnic cleansing had contributed to a toxic state of affairs.
Rabbis said that to eat the bread of a Samaritan was tantamount
to eating the flesh of a pig, the most detestable and repugnant act
imaginable to a Jew.

To travel through Samaria was bad enough, but then to find
Jesus speaking not just with a Samaritan, but a Samaritan *woman*,
had been shocking. Surely no good could come from this? And
yet, as they were still trying to process the significance of such radical behaviour, they began to see astounding signs of the impact
of Jesus' presence and work: 'Many of the Samaritans from that
town believed in him because of the woman's testimony . . .'

---

1. The account of a nineteenth-century traveller who visited this area
portrays a landscape that was both exquisite in its beauty and prolific in its
productivity: 'corn-fields dotted the more level places; and sparkling rills
danced and made music across our path': Thomson, A., 1882, *In the Holy
Land*, London: Nelson and Sons, p. 212.

(John 4:39). 'Open your eyes', Jesus says. 'See that God is at work here. See the signs of the Kingdom.'

No doubt there was an attractive vista laid out before them, but Jesus was drawing their attention to something more profound and important than the fields of corn. He was instructing them to use more than their physical sense of sight. He wanted them to use their capacity to discern what was going on; to understand the meaning and significance of what they were witnessing, as on another occasion when he rebuked them, 'You know how to interpret the appearance of the sky, but you cannot interpret the signs of the times' (Matthew 16:3). In telling them to 'open their eyes', he wanted them to wake up to a deeper reality, to engage all their God-given faculties, and recognise what was going on behind the physically obvious.

Boiling frogs

This directive to 'open your eyes and take a good look at what's right in front of you' is one that has had a major impact on my own thinking and priorities in recent years. You have probably heard the one about the frog and the boiling water. Folk wisdom has it (but please don't try this at home!) that a frog dropped into boiling water will jump out, but if placed in cold water that is then heated gradually, it will fail to register the change and remain until cooked to death. Whether or not this is factually accurate, the meaning is clear. Like frogs and other sentient creatures, we easily perceive changes that are stark and sudden. Gradual changes, on the other hand, often go unnoticed or disregarded. In 2007, I returned to the UK after working overseas for twelve years. It took me a while to realise that some of the changes that were obvious to me, as I came back after a long spell away, were often unnoticed or overlooked by many.

This book has come into existence not because I enjoy spending weeks in front of a computer monitor, but rather because I am convinced that we are living through a period of exceptional change and that, as Christians, we need to take seriously

Jesus' commandment to *open our eyes*, to discern and understand the significance of what is going on right under our noses. Even twenty years ago, when information technology was still in its infancy, Peter Drucker, the well-known writer and educator in the world of business, proposed that we were entering the kind of dramatic transformation that seems to occur every few hundred years in Western history. He suggested that in fifty years' time (or thirty from now) society will have so thoroughly rearranged itself that people who are born then will be unable to imagine the world in which their grandparents lived.[2]

Of course, the gradual and not-so-gradual changes in society are countless and diverse, but of particular interest to me, from the perspective of a Christian who had been out of the UK for more than a decade, were changes within the Church. By 'Church' (capital 'C') I mean the Christian community, 'the body of Christ' (1 Corinthians 12:27), rather than any particular organisation, institution or denomination. Some changes, which were sufficiently gradual as to go largely unnoticed by many, looked like an abrupt upheaval to me. I am talking about what one researcher has described as 'a haemorrhage akin to a burst artery',[3] the exodus from church congregations of hundreds of thousands of people.

Across different parts of the UK, the picture is mixed. In England there are some areas of significant growth within the church, which almost compensate for widespread decline. The result is that, after a lengthy period of decline, church attendance in England has levelled out. One example of growth is the dramatic development of some ethnic minority churches as a consequence of immigration to London and some other large cities. In fact, church attendance in London grew from just over 620,000 in 2005 to just over 720,000 in the seven years to 2012, an enormous

---

2. Drucker, P., 1993, *The post capitalist society*, New York: Harper Business, p. 1.

3. Brierley, P., 2000, *The tide is running out*, London: Christian Research, p. 236.

16 per cent increase.[4] Attendance at cathedrals has also increased in recent years.

Perhaps most encouraging for the long term, the strategy of planting new, culturally specific congregations, known as 'Fresh Expressions', is bearing considerable fruit. The Fresh Expressions movement describes itself as a 'form of church for our changing culture, established primarily for the benefit of people who are not yet members of any church [which] will come into being through principles of listening, service, incarnational mission and making disciples'.[5] Over 3,000 of these new forms of church now exist, spanning most church traditions in the UK.

However, despite these encouraging signs, the fact remains that there is widespread decline in attendance and membership beyond these areas of growth. In the five years between 2008 and 2013, the overall decline in church membership in the UK was about 5 per cent. Even this figure masks what was for some of the largest denominations a period of extraordinary decline. For example, membership of the Church of Scotland plummeted from 607,714 in 2000 to 415,705 in 2013. In 2007, the Christian charity, Tearfund, found that 33 per cent of people in the UK were 'dechurched'.[6] In Scotland, despite higher rates of church attendance than the UK as a whole, 39 per cent were dechurched. The situation in Wales was more shocking still, with a staggering 51 per cent dechurched.

Throughout the Western world the pattern is repeated. Reports from the Pew Research Center[7] in the USA and the Christian Research Association in Australia[8] both highlight similar trends of tumbling church attendance. The 2013 census in New Zealand

4. Brierley, P., 2014, *Capital growth: What the 2012 London church census reveals*, Tonbridge: ADBC, p. 3.

5. www.freshexpressions.org.uk/about/whatis.

6. This is an awful term, which focuses on what people no longer do, rather than what they currently are. However, it was used in that research to describe someone who previously attended church, but no longer does so.

7. www.pewforum.org/2015/05/12/americas-changing-religious-landscape/.

8. www.cra.org.au/why-some-churches-decline-while-others-grow/.

showed that fewer than 1.9 million people were affiliated with a church, compared with more than 2 million in 2006.[9]

Burning questions

So, the church is declining. Or is it? Clearly, overall attendance at Sunday morning services is decreasing. But what is happening to these people? Is the declining membership of many church denominations and institutions necessarily synonymous with a decline in Christian faith? What does this upsurge, of people who used to go to church but no longer do, actually mean? In books with dramatic and despondent titles such as *The death of Christian Britain*[10] and *God is dead*,[11] some academics have enthusiastically interpreted diminishing church attendance as clear indication of a rapid and irrevocable process of secularisation. But what if we take a look behind the statistics? What if, rather than focusing on the relatively easy task of counting bottoms on pews on Sunday mornings, we were to find out what 'dechurched' actually means for the individual people concerned?

Behind every statistic is a person with a unique story. The word dechurched tells us what they are not doing (i.e. attending church), but not what they *are* doing. It tells us what they are no longer part of, but not what they *are* part of. So who are these people? Have the hundreds of thousands of people who have disengaged from their local church congregation in recent years also turned away from God? Or are many of the so-called dechurched practising a churchless, but nonetheless genuine Christian faith? If, rather than wholesale decline, we are witnessing a trend away from the traditional institutional forms of church towards something different,

9. www.stats.govt.nz/Census/2013-census/profile-and-summary-reports/quickstats-culture-identity/religion.aspx.

10. Brown, C., 2009, *The death of Christian Britain: Understanding secularisation, 1800–2000*, Abingdon: Routledge.

11. Bruce, S., 2002, *God is dead: Secularization in the West*, Oxford: Blackwell.

what then are we to make of that? Is it something to fight against? Could it even be that one day we might look back on this time as a time when God was acting to bring about the kind of historic transformation that we seem to see every few centuries?

The journey towards answering these questions began for me a few years ago. It was Easter. What a stirring scene! Gathered in a natural amphitheatre with a stunning panorama of the still snow-covered Cairngorms before us and the sparkling waters of the loch below, the final rousing chorus of 'Thine be the glory' brought another Easter celebration to a joyful and expectant climax. 'Christ is risen', called out a booming voice from the midst of the loose semicircle of eighty or ninety people. Young and old, men and women, local residents and tourists, all replied in one voice, 'He is risen indeed!'

After twelve years away, working in South Asia, it was good to be back in this Highland village, the scene of my formative years as a Christian. As people gathered around the embers of the campfire and shared a simple breakfast of fish and bread, I had a sense of homecoming. It was good to be among friends; and not just friends, but brothers and sisters in Christ. However, scanning the crowd, I began to realise that a few faces were missing. People I was certain would want to be here, friends who I knew were deeply committed to the Christian faith and to this local church, seemed to be absent.

In the weeks that followed, I asked after some of the people who, to someone with the perspective that comes from a lengthy time away, were conspicuous by their absence on that Easter morning and the Sunday mornings that followed. Where were Bob and Jean? What about George, Margaret, Iain and Liz? In most cases, answers were not easily available. Some had moved away, but not many. A growing list (yes, I started a list – and it soon equalled the number of people who attended worship services on a Sunday morning) simply seemed to have drifted beyond the consciousness of members of the congregation. And then I started to bump into some of those whose presence I had missed. I met them in shops, on a train, while walking the dog, when queuing at the bank. There was so much to catch up on. We exchanged stories.

It became apparent that, for most of them, their Christian faith continued to be the mainspring of their lives. However, they did not attend church.

At first I was mystified. Surely, in all but exceptional circumstances, to be a Christian was to be part of a local church congregation? In my understanding, the local congregation was right at the heart of God's purposes. Surely the chief agent of God's mission in the world was the local congregation, and an important purpose of that mission was to grow and strengthen the local church? During a period at Bible College I had been stirred by the powerful vision of the local church portrayed by the great Scottish theologian and missionary to India, Lesslie Newbigin. He stated unequivocally that the local congregation was the 'primary reality' in terms of Christian influence in society, the 'only hermeneutic of the gospel'. Anything other than the local congregation was 'secondary', he asserted, and had potential to contribute to God's purposes only if it was 'rooted in' and leading back to a local church.[12]

I found myself wrestling with what seemed to be an irreconcilable contradiction between what I believed and what I was seeing with my own eyes. A short time later, I began working for the Church of Scotland. My role as Regional Development Officer led me to work with congregations throughout the north of Scotland and it didn't take long to realise that, not only was what I observed in my own community far from unique, but also it seemed to be the norm. I needed to understand what was going on and find release from what felt like an uncomfortable tension between long-held beliefs and the reality I was encountering.

Burst artery or iceberg?

I began to read all I could find related to church-leavers and so-called 'churchless faith'. Two books in particular had a profound

---

12. Newbigin, L., 1989, *The gospel in a pluralist society*, Grand Rapids, MI: Eerdmans, p. 227.

influence on my understanding. Each in its own way attempted to get behind the statistics of waning attendances and declining church membership. The first was *Gone but not forgotten*[13] by Philip Richter and Leslie Francis. This important publication explained the findings of the *Church Leaving Applied Research Project*. This was established in the 1990s 'to take seriously the specific problem of church-leaving within the social context of England and Wales'.[14] As well as exploring the reasons church-leavers gave for their departure, this rigorous research confirmed my suspicions that most leavers (about two-thirds according to Richter and Francis) continue to have a Christian faith.

Putting together the jigsaw of existing research seemed to suggest, then, that there were huge numbers of people living out their Christian faith without any ongoing relationship with a church congregation. For example, if Tearfund were accurate in estimating that 39 per cent of the people of Scotland were dechurched, and the findings of Richter and Francis – that only about one-third of leavers cited a loss of faith as their reason for exiting congregational life – reflected the situation in Scotland too, then the implication was that my friends who had lost contact with the local congregation were just the tiniest tip of the tip of an iceberg. In fact the available research seemed to suggest that in some places, especially rural areas, the 'tip of the iceberg' analogy applied more accurately to those who attended church services on a Sunday morning and that church-leavers made up a majority of Christians. The implication appeared to be that those counted in church censuses can be likened to the protruding tip of an iceberg: visible, but the smaller part of a larger whole; those who have ceased attending a church (with a small 'c', i.e. a local congregation), but remain part of the Church (with a big 'C', i.e. the global Christian community), may be compared to the largely invisible bulk of ice that forms the main mass of icebergs.

---

13. Richter, P. and Francis, L. J., 1998, *Gone but not forgotten: Church-leaving and returning*, London: Darton, Longman & Todd.

14. Francis, L. J. and Richter, P., 2007, *Gone for good? Church-leaving and returning in the 21st century*, Peterborough: Epworth Press, p. 19.

The metaphor of a haemorrhaging artery used by those observing the falling attendance at Sunday morning services[15] would be applicable if one's sole concern was the Church as an institution, an organisation. However, it seemed that the iceberg analogy was a much better illustration of the Church in terms of the people, the worldwide Christian community. With a large part not easily observed, counting and surveying only those who sit in pews on Sundays inevitably reveals a partial and misleading picture of the Church.

Despite all my reading, the discomfort caused by the contradiction between my understanding of the central role of a local congregation in the Christian life and the picture that was emerging from the available evidence was far from resolved. If church-leavers had experienced a catastrophic crisis of faith, their decision would have been more understandable to me. If, after ceasing regular involvement with a congregation, the faith of leavers withered and died, then all I had been taught about the indispensable purpose and functions of the congregation would have been confirmed. However, if the data was to be believed, neither of these scenarios was commonplace. And the distress I experienced in thinking about what the research seemed to imply was not just an intellectual unease. The difficulty in reconciling belief and reality was accentuated by a concern for the welfare of both church-leavers and the congregations they had left.

While the title *Gone but not forgotten* reflected a genuine concern of its authors for leavers and congregations alike, it seemed that *Forgotten but not gone* might have been more apt. The data suggested that, in most cases, the people who had disengaged from church congregations up and down the country had not *gone* anywhere. They still lived in the same homes, attended the same places of work and were part of the same social networks. They just didn't attend church any more. The church at an organisational level has focused little attention on these leavers. At the local level also it would seem that, all too often, they were quickly

---

15. Brierley, *The tide is running out*, p. 236.

forgotten. Richter and Francis found that 92 per cent of leavers reported that no-one from the congregation had talked with them about why they were not attending during the weeks after their church-going ceased.

It is generally considered good practice for organisations to conduct 'exit interviews' with staff when they leave for whatever reason. Businesses and charities alike listen carefully to clients, members or supporters when they decide to take their custom or interest elsewhere. Great value is attached to the perspective of these people; it represents a priceless resource for learning and continuous improvement. In failing to listen to those who are leaving congregations, churches not only lose a valuable opportunity to learn but, more importantly, often miss a chance to express the love of Christ at times of difficulty and transition.

Churchless faith?

The second book to have a significant influence on my thinking came from the other side of the world. The very title gave me a jolt, jarring my understanding of church and causing me to re-examine my assumptions about the place of the congregation in Christian life. Alan Jamieson's book, *A churchless faith*, is based on in-depth interviews with just over 100 church-leavers and fifty church leaders in New Zealand. Rather than viewing church-leaving as a problem to be solved, he came to recognise that, for many of the people he listened to, their decision to leave congregational life became a necessary and integral part of an ongoing journey of faith.

The title, *A churchless faith*, despite conveying accurately the experience of those Jamieson interviewed, grated against the raw nerves exposed by my struggles. Here were two words which, when 'faith' pertains to Christian faith at least, seemed contradictory. For me, as for many others, to be Christian and to be a church-goer, while certainly not one and the same, were intimately and inextricably intertwined. Intuitively, they belonged together. Juxtaposing the terms church*less* and faith seemed plain wrong. If ever I had seen one, Jamieson's title was an oxymoron: two incongruous concepts, lumped together; and, in this case, a theological misnomer to boot. And yet . . . hearing the stories of 'churchless Christians' interviewed by Jamieson, while they had become 'completely alienated from institutionalized forms of church',[16] it was equally clear that, in an important and vital way, they rightly understood themselves as part of the Christian community.

The word from which we get our English word 'church' and the Scots word 'kirk' literally means 'belonging to the Lord' and, as Jamieson listened to church-leavers describe their journeys of faith, it was clear that these were people who did indeed belong to the Lord; they were committed followers of Jesus Christ.

However, the term most commonly translated as 'church' in the New Testament is different. It is the Greek word *ekklesia*. Its root meanings contain the idea of being 'called out'. The word also had a use prior to being adopted by the Christian community. In a Greek city, the *ekklesia* was the gathering of all who were eligible to vote, an assembly of the town council. They were 'called out' from their homes by a town crier when communal discussion and decision-making were required. In an important sense the *ekklesia* only existed when it gathered. The early Christians took this word and enhanced its meaning so that, by the time the books of the New Testament were being written, it was used in several different ways.

Within the epistles of St Paul, *ekklesia* is often used to refer to the entire global and eternal population of Christian believers, both living and dead, as in what is sometimes called the universal church. In this sense there is only one church: the 'one, holy, catholic and apostolic Church' referred to in the ancient Christian creeds. At other times, *ekklesia* denotes the Christian community of a particular town or the actual assembly of believers when they are gathered together. Occasionally it is used to refer to a small group that gathered in a particular house, such as the *ekklesia*

---

16. Jamieson, A., undated, www.spiritedexchanges.org.nz/store/doc/A Churchless Faith.pdf.

that met at Priscilla and Aquila's house, which Paul greets at the end of his letter to the Romans.[17]

If the title of *A churchless faith* was jarring, the content was challenging too. Jamieson stated that 'the vast majority' of those he interviewed reported a lengthy and gradual process of consideration, questioning and withdrawal, lasting months or years, before they eventually left.[18] Of those he interviewed, most (94 per cent) had been in leadership positions within their congregation. The average time they had been involved as adults in congregational life was in excess of fifteen years. The majority indicated that they were now 'retaining their faith while leaving the church'.[19]

Digging deeper

With the exception of the two books I have just mentioned, I was disappointed with the quality of the literature I found on church-leavers. All too often it seemed that so-called research was, at best, well-intentioned but flawed, or, at worst, a façade for promoting pre-existing views. I have always been a fan of Sherlock Holmes and it seemed to me that some of the authors I encountered would have done well to heed his advice: 'It is a capital mistake to theorise before one has data. Insensibly one begins to twist facts to suit theories, instead of theories to suit facts.'[20] I began to see what Alan Jamieson meant when he suggested that this phenomenon of church-leaving is one where confusion, misunderstanding, stereotypes, and ignorance are rife.[21]

Good research is dependent on asking the right people the right questions. Sometimes it appeared that the questions in surveys had reflected more of the researcher's assumptions and prejudice

17. Romans 16:5.

18. Jamieson, A., 2002, *A churchless faith*, London: SPCK, p. 32.

19. Jamieson, *A churchless faith*, p. 15.

20. Conan Doyle, A., 1892, *The adventures of Sherlock Holmes*, London: George Newnes Ltd, p. 163.

21. Jamieson, *A churchless faith*, p. 17.

than the perspectives of church-leavers. One project I came across claimed to reveal new insights into the reasons why people left churches based on surveying 500 people. It sounded impressive. Who can question the views expressed by such a substantial sample? The insights were shocking. The findings sounded authoritative and were widely publicised in national newspapers and Christian magazines.[22] One report in *The Times*, typical of others at the time, ridiculed the apparently trivial reasons that drove people to leave congregations: 'It is not the big doctrinal issues. Typical arguments take place over types of buildings, styles of worship, youth work. If not that, then they argue over the flower rota.'[23]

On closer inspection, 98 per cent of the people who participated in this survey attended church regularly and more than 50 per cent of them had been in the same congregation for more than ten years. This means of course that what had really been discovered were *not* the reasons why people left church congregations; what was *actually* revealed were the perceptions of regular church-goers about why people leave congregations. This was a particularly stark and disappointing example of how poor research leads to weak understanding and misguided policy and strategy. In addition to the wide media coverage, these 'findings' went on to inform and shape the content of a major conference and gave birth to a book and training materials aimed at helping church leaders to 'close the back door of the church'.

The realisation that trivial issues were being treated as serious ones and that genuine, important ones were being totally ignored provoked me to dig deeper. The fact that simplistic and unsubstantiated explanations for such a huge and serious issue had been widely accepted impelled me to embark on the voyage of discovery on which I invite you to join me in this book. This was a journey for which I felt woefully unprepared. Had I known either the duration

---

22. www.christiantoday.com/article/uk.congregations.falling.for.trivial.petty.reasons.survey.finds/3772.htm.

23. Gledhill, R., 2005, August 25, 'Petty squabbles cause empty pews' in *The Times*. Retrieved from www.religionnewsblog.com/12068/petty-squabbles-cause-empty-pews.

or complexity of the journey, I would never have begun. Certainly I would not have dared to embark on the adventure alone.

Providentially, my early searching for companions led me to enrol as a doctoral student under the supervision of Professor Leslie Francis. As the author of *Gone But Not Forgotten*, one of the books that had already been an important source of inspiration and guidance, Leslie's wealth of experience in a variety of research approaches and the support of other students in the Centre for Studies in Rural Ministry[24] provided the expertise, encouragement and constructive criticism that I needed to launch out on what was to be a three-year expedition of listening to and learning from Christians who are not engaged with a church congregation. Along the route I have met some incredibly inspirational and impressive Christians. Listening to their stories has been an enormous privilege.

Researchers talk about 'deductive' and 'inductive' studies. A deductive approach sets out with an existing idea and tests it. Inductive research, on the other hand, assumes nothing; it begins by gathering as much information as possible and, keeping an open mind for as long as reasonable, looks for ideas and explanations to emerge. For my purposes, I wholeheartedly embraced this latter approach in a study that became known as *Faith journeys beyond the congregations*.[25]

The first challenge was to make contact with Christians who did not attend church. Articles in local newspapers and the use of social media turned out to be the most fruitful techniques for getting in touch with such people. It was surprisingly easy to find nearly 100 people who were willing to share their experiences. From this larger group I selected a cohort of thirty, about half men and half women, people from different generations who had had a variety of experiences of church. For example, the interviewees

---

24. The Centre for Studies in Rural Ministry is accommodated in Glyndwr University, Wales: www.arthurrankcentre.org.uk/mission-and-ministry/centre-for-studies-in-rural-ministry.

25. A report, *Faith journeys beyond the congregations*, is available for free download here: www.resourcingmission.org.uk/sites/default/files/downloads/Faith_journeys_beyond_the_congregations.pdf.

included folk who had left a congregation that they had been part of for a long time; others had disengaged from church when moving house; a few within the sample were committed Christians but had never been regular church-goers. It was not, of course, a random sample. Rather I was trying to get the full breadth of perspectives and experiences represented so that I would then know the right questions to ask a larger, random group.

With this group of thirty I asked them simply to share their personal story as far as it related to Christian faith and any experiences of church. Occasionally, a few prompts were needed to keep the story going or to clarify things, but in most cases their accounts flowed with minimal input from me. For those who had left congregations recently, the interview was often a cathartic experience as they shared raw emotions and experiences that they were still trying to process. Those who had been out of church for a longer time were usually more able to articulate an understanding of what they had experienced, having had, in some cases, many years to reflect and come to a considered understanding of all that had occurred. In addition to hearing what had led them away from congregational life, I was also keen to hear about their Christian journeying now.

All of this took place over several months in 2013 and resulted in nearly thirty hours of recorded interviews and almost 160,000 words of interview transcripts. Using some clever computer software and a system of picking out recurring issues and the matters which appeared to be most important to the interviewees, a number of themes emerged. These then were the foundation for two surveys of substantial and scientifically random samples.

The first, in 2014, focused on the north of Scotland (*Investigating the invisible church*);[26] the other, in 2015 (*Faith in Scotland*), tried

---

26. A report, *Investigating the invisible church*, is available for free download here: www.resourcingmission.org.uk/sites/default/files/downloads/Investigating the invisible church.pdf. A more comprehensive account of this research was published in the peer-reviewed journal, *Rural Theology*: 'A Survey of Christians in the Highlands and Islands who are not part of a Church Congregation', *Rural Theology*, 12(2), November 2014, pp. 83–95.

to shed light on the difference between rural and urban areas regarding church-leaving and Christian life beyond congregational involvement. In the 2014 survey, 2,700 people took part in a short telephone interview in order to identify people who were Christians, not attending a church congregation, and willing to participate in our research. Subsequently 430 people who fitted these criteria completed a detailed survey, comprising seventy-six questions about their experiences and perceptions. In the 2015 survey, 815 Christians who do not attend church participated in telephone interviews across five representative regions. These careful studies of reality, together with my own study of other research, form the backbone of this book.[27]

So, grab your ice axe because we're going to explore the iceberg that is the Christian community. You will need your aqualung too, because we shall be venturing into hidden depths as we take a careful look at the invisible and extensive mass that lies below the surface.

---

27. The findings of all these studies are freely available in a variety of articles, reports and papers in academic journals at www.resourcingmission.org.uk/resources/mission-research.

So what?
Questions and activities
for further reflection

'Behind every statistic is a person with a unique story.' Regardless of whether you are a regular church-goer or not, consider for a moment whether there is someone you know who is a Christian but not a church-goer? Could you ask them to tell you their story? Assure them that you will keep the conversation confidential. Listen carefully and in a non-judging way. How do they experience Christian fellowship? What were the main factors that led them to leave church – or not to engage with a congregation in the first place? You might want to buy them a copy of this book (cunning marketing strategy!).

The 'boiling frogs' analogy reminds us that significant changes can creep up on us unawares due to their gradual nature and our being too close to notice. If you have lived in the same community for some time, follow Jesus' instruction and 'take a good look at what's right in front of you'. Make a list of all the things that have changed over that period – visible things, but also less tangible changes that you detect. If you are part of a congregation you could do the same activity for your church. With either activity you might want to involve others, to get their perspectives too. You could work together to create a timeline which documents or illustrates the story of change. Ask yourself, why have these changes occurred? Are they, from your perspective, positive or negative developments?

If you are part of a church congregation, make a note of people you can think of who were involved previously, but no longer attend. Where are they now? Have they 'switched' to another congregation or are they no longer involved with a church? Have they retained their commitment to the Christian faith? Take a moment to pray for each person.

CHAPTER 2

Myths which masquerade as facts

Sometimes we encounter evidence which causes us to question our previously held opinions and revise our understanding. When it comes to trends regarding the Christian faith and churches, all is not as is sometimes assumed or portrayed. As King Solomon, famous for his wisdom, observed: 'Any story sounds true until someone tells the other side and sets the record straight.' Here, seven widespread views are reviewed in the light of reliable research and discovered to be more myth than fact.

The intelligent man is always open to new
ideas. In fact, he looks for them . . .
Any story sounds true until someone tells the
other side and sets the record straight.

Proverbs 18:15, 17

Mental maps

I would like you to take part in a short experiment. Can you please put this book down for a moment and point to where you think north is? Now think what went on in your mind between reading that I wanted you to point north and deciding which way to point. I've often asked groups of people to do this simple exercise in orientation. It's entertaining to see a room of a few dozen people pointing in a few dozen different directions! However, the main purpose is to make people aware that, in deciding where they thought north was, invariably, they consulted a kind of 'mental map'; typically they considered certain familiar landmarks or features, remembered the position of the sun, orientating themselves according to places they already knew.

During our lifetimes, we accumulate an impressive assemblage of mental maps. They are not just geographical maps either, but concepts or pictures of how things are – according to our experience of life so far. We build up impressions of others, inklings about the kind of people they are. We develop notions about political parties, organisations, goods made by particular manufacturers. Your emotional response to the mention of a Rolls Royce car will be quite different from your feelings about a three-wheeled Reliant Robin, even if you have never driven either.

Occasionally we find a mental map is challenged. Perhaps that person you thought was a saint turns out to be human after all, or the person who you always thought was so mean surprises you with an act of kindness and a smile, forcing you to redraw that particular map. About twenty-five years ago I went with a small group of friends on a mountaineering expedition to Peru. A couple of days' walk from a remote village we established a base camp, encircled by awe-inspiring mountains. Spectacular hanging glaciers tumbled down towards turquoise lakes. Herds of alpacas, Peru's diminutive woolly llamas, grazed the foothills around the camp. Over the next few days we explored the surrounding mountains and valleys, acclimatising to the rarefied air and prospecting for potential peaks to climb.

We had a map but, frustratingly, time and time again, we found that what it depicted and what reality presented were two quite different things. Lakes which shouldn't have been there definitely were. A river seemed to take a radically different course from the one portrayed on the map. In the dispute between map and reality, there was only ever going to be one winner. Reality trumps the map every time. We subsequently discovered that, some years earlier, an earthquake and associated landslides and avalanches had resulted in some significant changes to the terrain. Reality was right; the map was wrong; it needed updating.

Something deep within our human psyche means that once we have formed an idea or concept we like to hold on to it, even defend it. When our understanding is undermined or threatened by a contradictory idea, we experience discomfort or feel vulnerable. As Solomon, with his God-given wisdom, puts it, 'The intelligent man is always open to new ideas' (Proverbs 18:15). If your map comes into conflict with reality, change your map. If the compass needle points one way and you point another, think again. Indeed, Solomon exhorts us to be proactive in seeking out new information, fresh ideas, knowledge that will lead us into a more accurate understanding of reality and truth.

One of Solomon's supreme contributions to the generations and cultures that were to follow him was the concept of *audi alteram partem*. It has nothing to do with cars. It literally means 'hear the other side'. Or, as Solomon put it, 'Any story sounds true until someone tells the other side and sets the record straight' (Proverbs 18:17). Those three Latin words have become one of the most precious and inviolable principles of judicial systems around the world. As the judge in one ancient case noted, 'Even God himself did not pass sentence upon Adam before he was called upon to make his defence.'[1]

As we allow the empirical evidence to test some of the widely held assumptions and opinions about Christians who live their lives outside the traditional context of a church congregation, we must be open to any need to re-evaluate and amend our own understanding. In endeavouring to discern what is going on behind the statistics, we need to hear both sides of the story. To observe that people have 'gone' from church congregations without ascertaining why is lazy and uncaring. To fail to discover where they have gone and not to explore the nature of non-congregational Christian faith is negligent and short-sighted. Love, the hallmark of Christian community, compels us to listen to our brothers and sisters who are on a journey of non-congregational faith. *Audi alteram partem* – 'hear the other side' – a basic yardstick of wise judgement, demands that we make every effort to understand from all relevant perspectives.

Beginning with a global perspective and then zooming in to specific trends in the UK Church, let's explore some of the ideas that have been expounded as truth, but which empirical evidence undermines and challenges, revealing them to be myths that masquerade as facts. Let's allow evidence to evaluate anecdote. Let's enlist reliable data to assess the authenticity of assumptions and speculation.

Myth 1. It's all doom, gloom and decline

Despite the impression conveyed by Western media, the Church (capital 'C', the worldwide Christian community) is growing. The Church is always growing. It is growing in at least three different ways. It is growing in depth or holiness as people are changed through their encounter with Christ and the work of his Spirit; it

---

1. The King vs Chancellor, University of Cambridge (1722). Retrieved from www.duhaime.org/LegalDictionary/A/AudiAlteramPartem.aspx.

is growing in terms of its impact, the transforming actions of the Christian community in wider society; and, yes, it is growing in terms of the number of people who are followers of Jesus Christ.

Lifting our eyes from the situation in the UK for a moment, let's remember that at the end of the nineteenth century, about 3 per cent of the population of southern Africa was Christian. Of the more than 80,000 people who are embracing Christianity each day in the twenty-first century, it is estimated that about 34,000 live in that great continent of Africa. Today, approximately 63 per cent of people in southern Africa now identify themselves as Christians.[2]

In 1900, Korea had no Protestant church. Today, there are over 7,000 churches in the city of Seoul alone and about 30 per cent of the population confess Christianity as their personal faith. The People's Republic of China is officially an atheist country, but is on course to become the world's most Christian country within about fifteen years. We in Europe find the rate of church growth in a country like China difficult to comprehend. In 1950, China's Protestant community numbered about one million. By 2010, there were more than fifty-eight million Protestants in China. A leading expert on religion in China believes that this number will mushroom to around 160 million by 2025 and that, by 2030, China's total Christian population will exceed 247 million.[3]

Other faiths are growing too, of course, most notably Islam, but, however you choose to measure it, the Church, the worldwide community of Christians, is expanding, and that dramatic growth of Christianity is far from confined to these few examples.

The regions where the Church is ebbing are confined to Europe, regions dominated by the descendants of European ancestors,

---

2. Meyer, D., 2012, *Witness essentials*, Downers Grove, IL: Inter Varsity Press, pp. 32–33.

3. Professor Fenggang Yang, Purdue University and author of *Religion in China: Survival and revival under communist rule*, quoted in Philips, T., *The Telegraph*, 19 April 2014, 'China on course to become world's most Christian nation within 15 years'. Retrieved from www.telegraph.co.uk/news/worldnews/asia/china/10776023/China-on-course-to-become-worlds-most-Christian-nation-within-15-years.html.

such as North America, Australia and New Zealand – and the Middle East. So, paradoxical or ironic as it may seem, only the region of Christianity's birth and those nations whose culture and institutions are most strongly rooted in Christian heritage are seeing widespread decline in church congregations.

Myth 2. An inevitable slide into secularisation

The view of the most influential philosophers and economists of the nineteenth century – people such as Marx, Weber and Freud – was that the processes of modernisation and development would inevitably lead to a shrinking role for religion. It is a view still promoted by some academics, but one which is challenged by a growing surge of evidence to the contrary.

As we look around the world today, the Church is expanding in most regions. Growth has occurred on a scale that even the most prayerful and optimistic contemporaries of the nineteenth-century political economists could never have imagined, and some of the most dynamic growth is occurring in the context of exceptional economic expansion and development. Striking examples, in China and South Korea, have already been mentioned. In 2014, *The Economist* magazine reported that, as well as being a 'dynamo for economic growth', South Korea 'is also afire with faith'.[4] Brazil is another example of a nation where remarkable progress in health, education and prosperity has occurred in parallel with a dramatic burgeoning of the church. While it would be wrong to ignore the complexities that lie behind both development and church growth in these situations, the big picture certainly challenges the view that industrialisation, better health and widespread access to education inevitably lead to a decreased interest in spirituality and religion.

At least one of the most outspoken proponents of the idea that development will lead to secularisation has taken a U-turn in the

---

4. www.economist.com/blogs/economist-explains/2014/08/economist-explains-6.

face of the growing evidence base that argues to the contrary. The renowned Austrian sociologist, Peter Berger, spent most of his academic career in universities in the USA, where he was an ardent exponent of the idea that the world is on an irreversible journey into ever greater secularisation. He later conceded that the balance of evidence had convinced him of the folly of this theory and spent the latter part of his career suggesting that, far from being the engine of secularisation, modernisation was strengthening religion.[5]

Professor Grace Davie, perhaps the pre-eminent authority on religion in Europe, believes that those who understand the decline in church attendance as a one-way street to secularisation are making huge assumptions about what changing religious behaviour indicates and what it means for the future of churches and the wider Christian community. She believes that the role of the churches in western Europe has, in fact, been 'written off far too soon'.[6]

After the initial explosive growth of the Church which we read about in the New Testament, the story of Christianity is characterised by ebbs and flows, seasons of advance and periods of decline. There is no inevitability about the decline of churches. History shows that, especially at times of exceptional social change, churches need to respond in renewal and reform. Grace Davie points out that, far from being predetermined, continuing decline in church attendance depends to some extent on how churches respond. She draws a parallel with cinema going and attendance at football matches in the UK, both of which waned considerably in the latter part of the twentieth century, but which experienced a turnaround as cinemas and football clubs pioneered new ways of engaging with people, embraced new technology, and changed the ways in which they presented the same basic product.

---

5. Berger, P., 1999, *The desecularization of the world: The resurgence of religion in world politics*, Grand Rapids, MI: Eerdmans.

6. Davie, G., 2001, 'The persistence of institutional religion in modern Europe', in Woodhead, L. with Heelas, P. and Martin, D. (eds), *Peter Berger and the study of religion*, Abingdon: Routledge, p. 101.

The distinguished philosopher Charles Taylor has observed how changes in society sometimes lead to ordinary people feeling estranged from the 'spiritual style' of established religious institutions. The resulting decline in these institutions is often followed by reform movements which lead to the reinvigoration of faith as people develop other modes of Christian life and worship and 'live by their own spiritual style'.[7] He points, for example, to the innovative developments pioneered by the early Methodists in eighteenth-century England, the rise of Baptist churches in rural USA and the present-day rise of Pentecostal and Evangelical churches in Latin America.

As the ebbing of the tide precedes its resurgence, declining church attendances and membership can be the precursor of reformation and rejuvenation. Experts in managing change in commercial and charitable organisations have observed that, for change to take root and be beneficial, certain conditions must be present. These have been expressed in what is known as 'the change formula', and it applies equally in a church context:

$$C = D + V + FS + E > £$$

In everyday language, this means: Change = Discontent + Vision + First steps + Energy, all of which taken together must be perceived to deliver benefits greater than the cost involved (the 'cost' referring to all kinds of effort, loss, emotional expense, personal sacrifice etc.). Understood in these terms, a widening gap between the culture, language and concerns of established churches and those of the ordinary person can contribute to the preconditions for change, development and growth, as discontent with current forms of church creates energy for exploring or pioneering alternative expressions of Christian community.

---

7. Taylor, C., 2007, *The secular age*, Cambridge, MA: Harvard University Press, p. 455.

Myth 3. The end of Christendom is the end of Christianity

An event occurred on 28 October in the year 312 that has shaped the history, development and self-understanding of the church ever since. On that day, the forces of two Roman Emperors, Constantine I and Maxentius, clashed. It is impossible to overstate the significance of that battle. An historian who recorded the events soon afterwards, citing Constantine himself as his source, tells us that Constantine had a vision of a cross of light and the words 'in this sign, conquer'.[8] Constantine ordered his soldiers to mark their shields with a Christian symbol and, following their victory, attributed their success to the intervention of the Christian God. An arch that he built to commemorate the triumph still stands in Rome.

This victory, as well as occasioning the emergence of Constantine as the sole ruler of the Roman Empire, had momentous religious consequences. After decades of the harshest persecution imaginable, Christian worship was decriminalised. Property seized from Christians during his predecessor's reign was returned. Previously, Christianity had been a revolutionary movement and Christians the enemies of the state. Now they were legitimate, mainstream, their radical gospel message sanctioned by the highest authority in the land. What had been subversive and dangerous became not only respectable, but the approved imperial religion. State and church became intertwined. Christendom was born. A cultural watershed had been crossed. I'm using the term 'Christendom' here to refer to the era in which Christianity was accepted, largely without question, as the foundation of society and the explicit source of values for the majority.

In some ways this sounds like good news. Surely it was good that Christians were no longer fodder for lions and bait for gladiators? However, besides transforming the day-to-day experience of Christian believers, these changes had a profound influence on the church's self-identity. Instead of being a dissident movement within society, the church became conventional. Thereafter, to

---

8. Eusebius of Caesarea.

be Christian was the default position rather than a radical decision with potentially deadly consequences. In such a context,
the church inevitably acquired influence, authority, even control. As one noted theologian sees it, what had been an open city
on a mountain (referring to Matthew 5:14) became more like a
stronghold complete with fortifications and moats.[9] The Jesus-
movement became an institution.

Since the Enlightenment, and especially in recent decades, Christendom has withered and with it the assumption that Christianity
is the cultural backcloth for all else in the Western world, has gone.
The problem is that, while the concept of Christendom no longer
provides the overarching narrative of Western culture, it continues to define the self-understanding of many (perhaps even most)
churches. Rather than seeing the loss of cultural respectability as
an opportunity for a re-focusing of the church on the person and
message of Jesus, many mourn the passing of Christendom. A
desire for the Kingdom that Jesus spoke of and demonstrated is
sometimes confused with a longing for the church to recapture its
dominant and privileged position. Many of our churches have been
shaped by the assumptions of Christendom and find themselves
providing answers to questions that are no longer being asked.
Our Christendom-shaped churches find themselves detached from
our post-Christendom communities.

The fact is that the world is over Christendom. Now the church
must get over it too. The task that faces Christians in the Western
world is not to lament the passing of Christendom, along with
its associated privileges and concessions. Dare I say, let's rejoice
at its demise! Rather than grieving for the privileges and concessions that Christendom afforded the church, let's recognise the
increasing marginalisation of Christianity as a wake-up call to
remember our roots and our calling to be 'in the world but not of
the world'.[10] This is a moment to rediscover the challenging and
hazardous message of Jesus.

---

9. Buhlmann, W., 1982, *God's chosen peoples*, New York: Orbis Books,
p. 67.
10. John 17:15–16.

Sadly, many people, including many Christians, interpret the passing of Christendom as the passing of Christianity and the demise of the Church. However, the empirical evidence explored in this book shows that substantial numbers of those people who have disengaged from churches long to be part of a vital, revolutionary, compassionate movement of Jesus-followers such as existed pre-Christendom. Indeed, a yearning for authentic Christian community and a dedication to following Jesus lies at the heart of many of the accounts I have listened to from Christians whose search has taken them beyond the traditional congregational setting.

Myth 4. Decline in church attendance is synonymous with decline in Christianity

In terms of changing patterns of church involvement, Europe is unusual, the UK is exceptional, and Scotland and Wales are extreme. The drastic decline in attendance at church services and membership of local congregations is undeniable. Seven editions of *Religious trends*, published annually by Christian Research, from 1998 to 2008 documented plummeting church attendance in England. Yet more extreme reductions in similar figures for Scotland and Wales have already been highlighted. As explained in the previous chapter, the overall situation in England has stabilised, but this is the result of notable growth in certain kinds of church (ethnic minority, Fresh Expressions and cathedrals) that almost balances out continued decline in most traditional congregations.

There is also incontrovertible evidence that the proportion of the UK population that embraces Christianity is also reducing. While the fact that the various surveys use different methods makes it difficult to compare figures and map trends, census and survey findings do convey both a decrease in the proportion of people who identify themselves as Christian and an increase in the proportion who say they have no religion. Getting a handle on the true scale of this change is more difficult and complex than might be imagined. One study, for example, showed that 30 per cent of people who indicated in a survey that they had 'no religion', claimed a religious affiliation in another survey a year later. By asking a variety of other questions in the same surveys, the study also found that very few of these people who appeared to change their minds indicated any significant change in religious belief or practice![11]

So, if there is church decline and there are also fewer people saying that they are Christians, why might 'Decline in church attendance is synonymous with decline in Christianity' be a myth rather than a fact? The reason this is a myth is that the decline in church institutions (e.g. attendance and membership) is considerably more substantial than the decline in Christianity. There are substantial numbers of people who are disengaging from congregational life, but continuing to practise the Christian faith.

Although he is simplifying complex data, Stuart Murray is right when he points out in his book, *Church after Christendom*, that about 1.6 million people a year join churches in the UK, but 2.8 million leave; over 2,000 people leave churches every week in the UK; some of these die or move house, but 1,500 leave for other reasons.[12] Add to this the findings of the now extensive and rigorous research which is explored in this book – research that shows that a majority of those who have left congregations continue to be committed to their Christian faith – and we see that, while there is decline, the more significant change relates to how it is that people are expressing their faith. Christians who are not attending a church congregation in the traditional sense comprise a considerable and growing population.

---

11. Lim, C., MacGregor, C. A. and Putnam, R. D., 2010, 'Secular and liminal: Discovering heterogeneity among religious nones', *Journal for the Scientific Study of Religion*, 49(4), pp. 596–618.

12. Murray, S., 2005, *Church after Christendom*, Milton Keynes: Paternoster Press.

Myth 5. Christians who do not attend church are all 'church-leavers'

When tracking down potential interviewees for the first phase of my research, it surprised me to encounter people who were clearly devoted followers of Jesus Christ and yet had *never* been part of a church congregation. These were often men and women who had discovered the Christian faith either through an evangelistic course (e.g. Christianity Explored or Alpha) or through a visit to a Christian community (e.g. Iona, Taizé), but had not engaged with a church congregation since. They spoke of the contrast they found between the lively, interactive, and hospitable setting in which they had discovered the Christian faith and their experience of local congregations. In each case, these people have initiated or become part of a small informal group, where they continue to enjoy fellowship and explore faith together.

One lady, who discovered a personal Christian faith after visiting a Christian community, reported: 'I, with a friend, started a [name of particular Christian community] group in my house because [it] just really worked for me. That's been going for at least three years.' One young woman with three small children explained how she had not given Christianity much thought until a friend invited her to a Christianity Explored course. She had many questions and welcomed the opportunity to ask them. As the course progressed, she 'became captivated by the person of Jesus' and by the end felt as though she was 'launching out on a huge adventure with Jesus as guide'. She visited local churches, but found a radical contrast to the vibrant, informal, and participative setting of the group of which she had been part. She also found that church attendance with her children was challenging. She meets occasionally with two friends, who were also on the Christianity Explored course, to share experiences and pray together.

The two surveys conducted as a follow-up to these interviews have confirmed the existence of a not insignificant population of Christians with no regular experience of church congregations. In northern Scotland, 15 per cent of people identifying themselves as

Christian but not church-going had *never* been regularly involved with a congregation. The rest of Scotland had a larger proportion of people (19 per cent) who identified themselves as Christians who had never attended church regularly. So, the fact is that most Christians who do not attend church are 'church-leavers', but not all.

If you find yourself thinking 'Yes, but what do all these people mean when they identify themselves as Christian?' read on, as that is an issue addressed in the following chapter.

Myth 6. *If congregations do the right things, leavers will become returners*

One of my favourite cartoons by Dave Walker, the creator of the excellent illustrations in this book, is titled 'How to make church brilliant'. Like most of his cartoons, there is enough exaggeration to make it entertaining, but sufficient basis in truth to ensure that, as our smile fades, we are provoked to some serious soul-searching. The cartoon shows myriad ideas for 'jazzing up' your congregation: beds are provided 'for those who find the service times a bit early', a 'dynamic preacher' balances on the lectern on one hand, and a kiosk serves a generous selection of drinks and snacks. It is a seductive idea that, if we adopt certain best practices or emulate the methods of growing churches, our congregation will acquire an irresistible, magnetic allure to those who currently show no flicker of interest.

Like many myths, there is a kernel of truth. There *are* certain features which are associated with healthy, growing congregations: some, in common with any kind of community, involve the fostering of strong relationships and effective communication; others are distinctively Christian, such as keeping Christ at the centre, nurturing faith and maintaining an outward focus. However, the data shows that the majority of 'churchless Christians', whether they were previously church-goers or not, are contentedly non-congregational. They are not waiting for their local church to make the necessary changes; only a small proportion of people are eager to engage with any congregation at all. Rather, they indicate that they prefer to live out their faith without reference to religious institutions. My own research in Northern Scotland found that just under a third of non-congregational Christians agreed with the statement, 'Not being involved in a traditional church congregation frees me to pursue what I believe is my Christian calling.' Most feel part of the wider Church. In one of the strongest responses among the seventy-six questions in the 2014 survey in northern Scotland, most agreed with the statement, 'I feel part of the worldwide Christian community.'

Survey responses from 'churchless Christians' who remain open to the possibility of returning to congregational life highlight two main factors which might encourage them to do so. First, the data suggests that there is a contingent for whom accessibility is a key concern. Especially among the elderly and people with health difficulties, there are those who would like to attend church regularly, but who find that they are unable to do so. In Scotland, 14 per cent of 'churchless Christians' who demonstrated that their faith was of great importance to them indicated that they would like to be part of a congregation but were prevented from doing so by issues of health. Second, there are others, who state that a 'different style' of church from what is currently available in their local area could lead to them becoming part of a congregation.

The *Faith in Scotland* survey in 2015 found that about 30 per cent of those Christians who are not currently church-goers would be open to join a congregation if there were other expressions of church available in their area. On the whole, these people would appreciate more informal expressions of church and, crucially, opportunities to ask questions and explore doubts. In the Highlands and Islands, for example, 8 per cent of all those who identified themselves as Christians but not church-goers said that they would welcome the opportunity 'to join a small group of Christians who meet in homes and discuss faith and life together'.

However, although there are appreciable numbers of people who are open to returning to congregational life, they are still the minority. The general suggestion that 'making church brilliant' will 'bring the prodigals home' runs counter to the evidence.

It is a myth; beguiling, but without basis. The fact is that most Christians living beyond church congregations find the lack of institutional ties liberating, a situation that positively enables their Christian vocation.

Myth 7. Churchless Christians are driven by consumerism

There is a widespread perception that many who are Christians, but not church-goers, are what has been dubbed 'spiritual butterflies'. The suggestion is that such people have so absorbed the spirit of consumerism that pervades our culture that they flit from church to church, 'shopping' for the congregation that best suits their requirements. Never satisfied, failing to find the perfect church, they literally 'shop till they drop'. Again, like so many myths, there is no doubt that this contains elements of truth. To suggest that Christians are unaffected and untainted by the powerful engine of consumerism that lies at the heart of Western cultures would be naïve. Of the thirty non-church-going Christians I interviewed initially, most described experiences of multiple denominations. However, most of their switching had been prompted by house moves rather than personal preference. Careful analysis of UK census data shows very low rates of 'switching' affiliation between denominations compared with other parts of the world (especially the USA). Analysis carried out by the University of Essex concluded that the amount of 'switching' is small in absolute terms and minor when compared with the incidence of church-leaving.[13]

The suggestion that many people flit from church to church on a whim fails to recognise the soul-searching, anguish and grief that often characterise church-leaving. Likewise, to suggest that a compulsion rooted in consumerism drives many who eventually disengage from congregational life fails to acknowledge the emotional complexity involved. Most church-leavers describe

---

13. Voas, D., (2006, March), 'Religious decline in Scotland: New evidence on timing and spatial patterns', *Journal for the Scientific Study of Religion*, 45(1), pp. 107–18, abstract.

how a sense of duty, commitment, fear or guilt constrained their behaviour, preventing them from disengagement for some considerable time. Most of the interviewees within my own research saw their decision to leave church congregations in relation to a journey of inner change and outer circumstances, factors over which they had, at most, only partial control. The data indicates that choices to switch, leave or not engage with a church congregation are more of a 'wrench' than a 'flit'. Those who are motivated primarily by simple, rational, consumerist preferences are the exception rather than the norm. Rather, the evidence points, in most cases, to the decision-making processes being intensely personal, rooted in the person's journey of discipleship, often influenced strongly by deep changes within the individual.

The power of myths

The pioneer anthropologist, Claude Lévi-Strauss, studied the function that myths have in our thinking and behaviour. He maintained that the role of myths in influencing our understanding and conduct is largely unconscious.[14] He also explains how one important function of myths is to protect the tribe, to safeguard them from outside challenges. Perhaps, on some subconscious level, the ideas that have been exposed as myths in this chapter have arisen to defend the understanding that the traditional church congregation is the sole orthodox context in which to practise the Christian faith and that divergence from this is dangerous and heretical. As we continue to explore and reflect on the evidence regarding changes in the Christian community, let's continue to keep in mind the wisdom of Solomon: 'The intelligent man is always open to new ideas. In fact, he looks for them . . . Any story sounds true until someone tells the other[15] side and sets the record straight.'

---

14. Lévi-Strauss, Claude, 1964, *Mythologiques I–IV* (trans. John Weightman and Doreen Weightman), *Le cru et le cuit* (*The raw and the cooked*, 1969), p. 12.

15. Proverbs 18:15 and 17.

So what?
Questions and activities
for further reflection

Do you recognise 'The end of Christendom' described in this chapter? What evidence would you point to in support of your answer?

'The fact is that the world is over Christendom. Now the church must get over it too.' What might it mean for the church to 'get over' Christendom?

'One important function of myths is to protect the tribe.' Consider carefully whether there are ways in which your own opinion or perspective regarding church in general or churchless Christians or wider society may comprise myths designed to protect you or your 'tribe'.

Remember the change formula: C = D + V + FS + E > £ ? It states that, for change to occur, there must be a degree of discontent (D) and a vision (V) of a preferred future. Then there needs to be clarity about the first steps required (FS) and sufficient energy (E). People need to believe that the benefits are greater than all the costs. Are you aware of 'discontent' within a community or a church that you are familiar with? If so, use the change formula to analyse the situation. What prevents change from happening or what would be required to initiate positive change?

CHAPTER 3

Stereotypes, generalisations and prejudice

We all have strategies for making sense of the complexity of life. One tactic, largely subconscious, is to simplify the world by means of some intellectual shortcuts. When it comes to people, we can't possibly know everyone's story – even less understand the intentions of their hearts – so we construct generalisations based on our own experiences and what we pick up from others. This chapter unmasks some commonplace assumptions about Christians who are not church-goers – and compares these with their own perceptions.

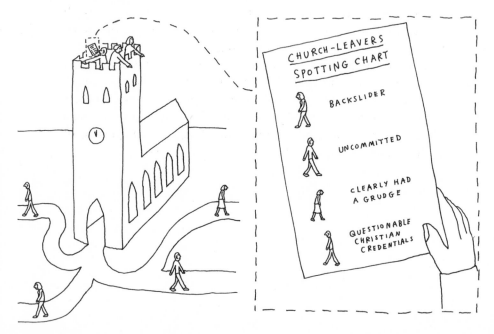

The LORD doesn't see things the way you see them. People judge by outward appearance, but the LORD looks at the heart.

1 Samuel 16:7

We all do it, but . . .

The contrast between the selection of Saul as the king of Israel and the appointment of his successor, King David, is instructive. Saul was an obvious choice. His face fitted. Nobody better matched the widely held image of a first-rate king. He was tall, brave, 'as handsome a young man as could be found anywhere in Israel',[1] charismatic and an effective warrior. However, as time went on, other aspects of his character surfaced. He was disobedient, egotistical, and developed into a self-aggrandising tyrant.

Again and again his life showed him to be lacking in the fundamental qualities required for someone appointed to a sacred position of trust. Unsurprisingly, the people of Israel and the prophet Samuel grew increasingly exasperated. God himself 'was grieved that he had made Saul king over Israel' (1 Samuel 15:35, NIV). However, despite all the suffering and sorrow caused by Saul's selection, as Samuel began to search for his replacement, we read that he was tempted to appoint a successor based on the most superficial of evidence. As he met David's eldest brother, Eliab, he was seduced by first impressions, swayed by outward appearance. Samuel, God's prophet, a frail human being like us all, was certain that Eliab must be the one: 'Surely the LORD's anointed stands here' (1 Samuel 16:6).

Fortunately, in his incomparable mercy, God, who 'looks at the heart', discerns character and knows the end from the beginning, intervened. He shared his divine perspective with Samuel. It must have been difficult for Samuel to accept this divine insight, for it meant amending his assumptions, questioning the stereotype of

---

1. 1 Samuel 9:2.

the ideal king, and embracing a radically different perspective. Having considered the suitability for the throne of all but one of Eliab's brothers, Samuel faced David who, as the youngest, was no more than a youth. As the last son in a society grounded in the primacy of the first-born, he was a nobody: his ethnic pedigree was flawed, as his great-grandmother was Ruth, a Moabite immigrant. Then the Lord said, 'he is the one'. At that moment, stereotypes crumbled, assumptions dissolved, prejudice evaporated.

Stereotypes are dangerous. When we view others through the distorting lens of stereotypes we reveal our own prejudice. Whatever your opinions about the previous incarnation of the quirky, irreverent, car-focused TV programme, *Top Gear*, it was hugely successful. At the time of the programme's suspension in early 2015 it had an estimated global audience of 350 million. The presenters' edgy and maverick style deliberately courted controversy, often landing them in hot water, as they criss-crossed the line between light-hearted humour and deliberate, headline-grabbing, ratings-boosting, offence. Perhaps the most notorious hullabaloo was sparked in 2011 when one host likened a Mexican sports car to 'a lazy, feckless and flatulent oaf with a moustache, leaning against a fence asleep, looking at a cactus with a blanket with a hole in the middle on as a coat' – and then said it mirrored Mexico's national characteristics. Predictably, among many others, Mexico's ambassador to the UK felt insulted by such stereotypical generalisations, describing them in his letter to the broadcaster as 'outrageous, vulgar and inexcusable insults'.

But we all do it. Don't we? Generalise, I mean; embrace and approve stereotypes. On one level we need stereotypes. Anthropologists tell us they exist in all cultures and serve an important purpose. In a complex world they provide a kind of shorthand, as we ascribe to individuals the characteristics of others whom we have met or, more often, heard about second-hand . . . or third-hand . . . or fourth-hand. In addition to our own experiences, rumour, hearsay and the media play powerful roles in shaping stereotypes. Add to this the fact that they are usually generated subconsciously, and it becomes easy to understand how stereotypes evolve and take on a self-perpetuating life of their own while we remain largely unaware.

Stereotypes develop when we ignore differences between individuals. Rather than embracing the complex reality that all individuals are created unique and have many facets to their personality, we accept a generalised, homogenised illusion, which seems to resonate with what we have heard or been told. The danger of using the shorthand of stereotypes is that we begin to believe they are true. In a curious twist of psychological behaviour known as 'confirmation bias', we absorb information which reinforces our stereotypes and ignore evidence which challenges them. Imagine the impact of this phenomenon: left unchecked or unchallenged it leads to, among other things, the polarisation of opinions and the illogical persistence of discredited beliefs.

Stereotypes may of course have a germ of fact at their core. However, even when they are not *untrue*, they are always *incomplete*. There is any number of stories to be told about any individual or group, church, business, club or nation. Each adds a greater depth of understanding. However, a stereotype makes one story into the *only* story. Chimamanda Ngozi Adichie, the remarkable Nigerian novelist, calls this the 'danger of the single story': 'Show a people as one thing, as only one thing, over and over again and that is what they become . . . the single story robs people of dignity.'[2] Although now a critically acclaimed writer (her novel, *Half of a Yellow Sun*, received the 2007 Orange Prize for Fiction), she tells how her American college professor judged her writing as 'lacking African authenticity'. On questioning the meaning of this assessment, she discovered that her stories failed to fit the stereotype he held of Africa: beautiful animals, poverty, senseless wars and AIDS. Her characters were not foreign enough; they were middle-class professionals who drove cars; they were not starving and were, therefore, 'not authentically African'!

As we continue our journey towards greater understanding of Christians who are not church-goers, let's determine to root out lazy stereotypes, question cherished assumptions, and expose prejudice for the affront that it is. May we learn the lesson that

---

2. Talk filmed for the TED internet-based channel in July 2009: www.ted.com/talks/chimamanda_adichie_the_danger_of_a_single_story?language=en.

served Samuel well as he held the fate of the Israelite nation in his hands – a lesson he had learnt under the tutelage of Eli the priest: as we review evidence and hear genuine voices, may we learn to listen for the divine voice.

Stereotype 1. The loner

It is a basic tenet of the Christian faith that, just as we are called into communion with Jesus Christ, so we are also called into relationship with other Christians. It is striking that when asked to teach his disciples how to pray, Jesus responded, 'When you pray, say, "Our Father . . ."'. Not 'My Father', but 'Our Father'. The moment we acknowledge God as Father, we also become part of a vast worldwide family with a multitude of sisters and brothers. The word used in the New Testament that we often translate as 'fellowship', *koinonia*, conveys the idea of a deep sharing in something that we have in common. This sharing demands a profound mutuality, as insisted upon in the many 'one another' exhortations of the New Testament: 'be devoted to one another' (Romans 12:10); 'serve one another' (Galatians 5:13); 'carry one another's burdens' (Galatians 6:2), to mention but a few.

In recent centuries, this Christian calling to fellowship with brothers and sisters has generally been interpreted in terms of commitment to a local church congregation. A verse from the letter to the Hebrews (Hebrews 10:25) is often employed as an appeal to 'go to church'. Indeed, some translations say as much: 'You should not stay away from the church meetings' (ICB); 'Let us not neglect our church meetings' (TLB); 'And let us not hold aloof from our church meetings' (Phillips). However, this is actually another 'one another' passage. The emphasis is not so much on the gathering, but on its purpose and the quality of the experience enjoyed by participants. We are to meet with others in such a way that we 'spur one another on towards love and good deeds' (v. 24) and 'encourage one another' (v. 25). If the stress was on congregating together, the writer had another word that he could have used. I won't get into the complexities of linguistics here, but suffice it to say that the difference between the word that the writer could have used, a word which is very common in the New Testament, and the word he chose to use can be likened to the difference between a bag of pebbles and a bunch of grapes. Both are superficially similar, of about the same size and shape. However, whereas the pebbles are a collection of unrelated, inanimate objects, lifeless, hard and cold, the grapes are in an organic relationship, of the same vine, growing together.

Of the people I have interviewed, all continued to affirm their need for gathering with other Christians and recognised the inherent opportunities in such a context for mutual encouragement and 'spurring one another on to love and good deeds'. As we look at people's experiences of leaving congregations, one of the striking things is their hunger for fellowship. On leaving a traditional congregation, the first thing many do is to seek out opportunities for meeting with other believers. Ironically, some of the most common reasons given for their reluctant departure from congregational life relate to the frustration and disappointment of not finding there the very qualities extolled in the New Testament as the touchstones of Christian fellowship. Interviewees spoke of a lack of love, a coldness and superficiality more to be expected of pebbles than grapes. Most interviewees described how, having ceased church-going, they had formed friendships or linked into informal groups which had Christian fellowship as an important part of their purpose. I'll let them tell you in their own words. 'We've . . . been meeting occasionally with some other couples that have come out of the church' was a typical statement. Another interviewee, a young woman who, after ceasing church attendance, began to invite other 'churchless' Christians to gather in her home, reported,

I stopped going to church but still needed some Christian fellowship, and that's why I asked us all to get together for the house group, because I was still needing something but I was aware of other people still needing somewhere where they could meet and talk, other friends that had stopped going to church or were feeling uncomfortable in the church family, building, whatever.

By 'house group' she meant an informal group gathering in her home for Christian fellowship with no link to any congregation. Most 'churchless' Christians described their main opportunities for fellowship as taking place in homes or public gathering places such as cafés. Only where numbers exceeded what could be comfortably accommodated in these places did the group begin to meet elsewhere. For example, one interviewee reported, 'We meet in a shop . . . There can be up to 15 people there on a Sunday morning. It's a very small group. Many folk would just call it a house group.'

A few interviewees described what might be called 'long-distance fellowship' as their main source of spiritual nurture and accountability. So, one person explained, 'What helps me most is an *Anam Cara* [a 'soul friend' in the Celtic tradition] who although in [a place several hundred miles away] is a great help . . . I am a long-distance parishioner of [name of a Christian community].' A number of people mentioned that the internet had been helpful in linking them to other Christians. One person who finds gathering in groups very difficult due to mental health challenges reported how helpful online churches such as www.stpixels.com had been; others mentioned webcasts and opportunities to join worship remotely. Several interviewees mentioned how listening to a worship service on the radio or on television had become highly valued since they disengaged from a congregation. A few did this as a shared activity with others: 'we meet in a home in [name of village] in the morning and we tune in to [recorded service] or listen to a DVD and join in.'

Stereotype 2. The 'backslider'

The oft-quoted story of Charles Spurgeon was referred to on several occasions, both in interviews I conducted and in focus groups I met with to reflect on the findings of the research. Apocryphal or otherwise, the story goes that Spurgeon was visiting a man who said that he was a Christian but did not believe he needed to go to church. Without saying a word, Spurgeon took the tongs from the hearth-side and removed one coal, setting it in the corner of the fireplace away from the others. It soon went out, and the man got the message: the coals in a fire need each other to stay hot and Christians need the fellowship of other Christians to keep them spiritually alive. The story has generally been quoted to reinforce the notion that to leave a church congregation is to step on to a slippery slope leading to loss of faith. However, the data suggests that personal Christian faith is more resilient than we often credit. One interviewee, referring to Spurgeon's illustration and describing a response to friends who had expressed their concern that he was 'backsliding', explained his belief that God had challenged him to withdraw from congregational fellowship and deepen his relationship with God and also with his wife:

It was like he [God] was wanting to take me out for a period, and [it] was actually he himself that was going to make me glow . . . [rather than] depending on being part of that fellowship, that fire, that he's wanting me to glow in my own right, outside the fire really. He wanted to do a work in me outside that . . . Sometimes I think we get built up, but how do we stand when we are out of the fire? And we all have times when we are isolated and on our own and we have bad times and it's like 'I want you to be strong, [person's name], even in those times.' You know, it's a bit like Jesus in the wilderness and it's a test of your faith, how strong you can be even when you're not getting buoyed up by fellowship.

Several interviewees reported that their faith life had diminished since they ceased regular congregational engagement. Typically, they described finding it difficult to maintain spiritual disciplines. One person, for example, reported, 'I've found it harder to read my Bible as much . . . I suppose I've found it harder to pray . . . But it hasn't made me feel further from God or more remote.' However, most people who had once been regular church-goers reported that, in retrospect, their faith journey had been positively impacted by disengagement from the congregation of which they were previously a part. So, while comments such as 'I do miss the fellowship' were not uncommon, most described a sense of relief after what, for most, had been a prolonged period of struggling and then soul-searching at the prospect of disengaging from the congregation. The following example epitomises the kind of experience many interviewees described: 'It was a wonderful relief when I realised I was free to walk away from the churches in which I had tried so hard to conform, but wasn't flourishing . . . ' One married couple described how their disengagement from church had led to a deepening of their relationship with one another and a deepening of their devotional life: 'It's been good in building up a relationship with God individually, but it's also been good for our relationship with one another.' A few even expressed concern for the well-being of friends who remained in regular involvement with a church congregation, but were struggling:

One of the things we keep encountering is a sense of a watershed that's developing . . . It feels as if God is presenting the church with a choice of either you change and you accept all the risks that go with that change, or you cling on to what's familiar even while it's dying . . . And a number of people that we know have chosen to cling on and have lost even the confidence they had because it feels like the sense of desperation is increasing.

In view of the widely held belief that to leave a church congregation is to backslide, it is ironic that the experience of many church-leavers suggests that a motivating factor in disengaging from a congregation is their desire to grow in Christian faith – and finding the congregational context unhelpful in that. Other researchers report similar findings. The *Church Leaving Applied Research Project*[3] found that 37 per cent of those under 20 and 23 per cent of those over 20 agreed that, 'The church was no longer helping me grow'; Jamieson's work in New Zealand found that the congregations his interviewees had experienced tended to

---

3. Richter, P. and Francis, L. J., 1998, *Gone but not forgotten: Church-leaving and returning*, London: Darton, Longman & Todd.

emphasise coming to Christian faith, but then had little to offer for the rest of the journey.[4]

Stereotype 3. The petty-minded

One of the most unfortunate and potentially hurtful views about church-leavers is that they are people who leave congregations after petty disputes or for reasons that are considered to be trifling by others in the congregation. As mentioned in the first chapter, this view has been reinforced by poorly executed research claiming to show that a range of inconsequential issues lie at the root of people's decision to leave congregations. 'UK Congregations Falling for Trivial and Petty Reasons, Survey Finds' was one headline prompted by this flawed study.[5]

Remember again the wisdom of Solomon: 'Any story sounds true until someone tells the other side and sets the record straight' (Proverbs 18:17). Recent and more rigorous research shows that it's not usually the case that church-leavers walk away for trivial reasons; it also suggests possible reasons why leavers themselves and those who remain sometimes have diametrically opposing views of why people leave congregations. These studies provide an alternative narrative – one that has emerged from data gathered from church-leavers themselves, rather than having arisen from the views of people still engaged with congregations.

This alternative explanation has two aspects. First, the lengthy period of frustration or disappointment that usually precedes disengagement leads to a perception by church-leavers that they disengaged for reasons that were serious and significant and that the decision was only arrived at after prolonged deliberation. Second, the fact that there are often 'tipping points' – incidents or situations that lead someone who has been struggling for some time to finally leave – may explain the perception of some of those

---

4. Jamieson, A., 2002, *A churchless faith*, London: SPCK, p. 146.
5. Blake, D., 2005, 'UK congregations falling for trivial and petty reasons, survey finds' at www.christiantoday.com/article/uk.congregations.falling.for.trivial.petty.reasons.survey.finds/3772.htm.

who remain in the congregation. Having witnessed an apparently minor incident or issue seeming to provoke a disproportionate reaction – and being unaware of the long-term nature of the leaver's frustrations – it is no surprise if they believe that they have witnessed an over-reaction to a relatively inconsequential matter. What they are unaware of is that what they have observed is actually an example of the idiomatic 'straw that breaks the camel's back'; a seemingly minor matter leading to a reaction that appears unpredictably major and sudden from their perspective, because of the cumulative effect of numerous preceding circumstances.

Although most come to see their disengagement from church in a positive light, the process is often bruising. The voices of church-leavers convey the pain that the significant losses involved often give rise to. A sense of being misunderstood can induce deep personal anguish that, for some, impacts their physical health and mental well-being. One young man, describing the concluding stages of his struggles with a church congregation, told me, 'I found it very difficult to worship and after a while I just had to leave . . . I got terribly depressed about the situation – it made me quite ill, night-mares, couldn't sleep . . . ' An older man who had been in a position of church leadership for more than three decades recounted: 'I was finding I wasn't sleeping well, I was finding that I was having very uneasy feelings and uneasy relationships within the church.' A young woman who had recently left a congregation after some years of disappointment with what she perceived as 'superficial . . . going through the motions week after week' confessed to struggling with feelings of guilt: 'I've grown up always going somewhere on a Sunday morning, it feels really weird and kind of wrong.'

The nature of people's 'exit routes' from church congregations, both their inner personal journey and the outward circumstances and behaviour, is explored in greater depth in the next chapter.

Stereotype 4. The uncommitted

I have heard it said, and perhaps you have too, that, in the past (the 'good old days' maybe), people just 'knuckled down', per-severed, and rode out the storms, the inevitable ups and downs of life in any church congregation. However, while there are certainly people who attend a church for a short time and decide that it is not for them, the empirical evidence is clear that many of those who once attended church regularly, did so diligently for many years before leaving. My own data from a random sample in the north of Scotland found that about a quarter of leavers had attended church regularly for more than twenty years; about half attended for more than a decade. The data from the rest of Scotland showed that the average time people had attended church before leaving was over fifteen years, with women more likely to hang in for longer (nearly seventeen years) than men (just over thirteen years). Here, then, is a group of people who, on the whole, have demonstrated considerable commitment over a significant period.

Just as Alan Jamieson found in his interviews with church-leavers in New Zealand, in my own research I encountered many people who, in addition to attending church for many years, had also held leadership roles during much of that time. Indeed, some of those I interviewed had been significantly involved in congregations for decades. For example, one recently retired man reported:

I was born within a Christian family, my parents were obviously church-goers and at an early age I was encouraged to go to church . . . I went to the Sunday School, which was called Junior Church – that was in the morning. By the time that I was a young teenager, I was also going to Crusaders, which was an afternoon Bible Study and by the time I was 13 or 14 also involved in an evening youth group at the church, so I was therefore going to church in the morning, going to Crusaders in the afternoon, going to Church and the youth group in the evening as well on a Sunday . . . By the time I was 16, we had in the [name of denomination] what we call Junior Membership of the church and I became a Junior Member. I became very involved in the church in my late teenage years and early 20s – I became the leader of the Junior Church . . . At the age of 24 I became an Elder in the church . . . I was the youngest Elder that they had ever had in the church and I continued to work within that role.

This man continued his deep commitment to the local congregation and served in a leadership role until, in his late fifties, after a few years of excruciating deliberation, he resigned as an Elder and left the congregation. His reasons were complex and will be explored in a future chapter, but nobody could suggest that his commitment had been anything other than exemplary.

Stereotype 5. The incomer

The UK, as in the world as a whole, has an increasing proportion of the population living in towns and cities. Over 80 per cent of the UK population now lives in urban areas – and this is increasing. However, apart from some notable exceptions, this does not mean that there is a corresponding depopulation of the countryside. Indeed, the last two decades have seen a net migration into rural areas. This may sound like a contradiction, but is clarified when one considers that the urban population is increasing faster than the rural, but rural areas are also becoming more populous, as a steady trickle of people opt for the 'good life' or 'retire to the country'.

In the discussion about declining church congregations and the emergence of 'churchless faith' in the countryside, one stereotype that has emerged is the 'incomer' who finds the local church not to their liking. The notion has some logical underpinning and there will be examples that fit the oversimplified cliché: the 'city slicker', used to driving past ten churches en route to their preferred congregation, finding the single or few congregations within reasonable reach of their new rural abode to be claustrophobic, unexciting, or antiquated. However, you guessed it: the facts convey a different picture. For example, my research in the Highlands and Islands (and you don't get much more rural than that), found that about half of the Christians who are not involved with a congregation have lived in the region their whole lives and that over 80 per cent have lived there for over twenty years. Most of the congregational leavers in rural areas have left local churches that they were part of for many years; they are not recent arrivals. Those who fit the incomer stereotype are the exceptions, a tiny minority.

Stereotype 6. *The Christian in name only*

Some academics have made the bold and unsubstantiated assertion that those who explain their lack of church involvement by any reason other than a lack of belief are either fooling themselves or fooling the researchers; they are keen to emphasise that responses to surveys related to church involvement are unreliable due to being 'shaded by politeness and guilt'.[6] Others have claimed that the faith of people who claim to be Christian but who are not engaged with a church congregation is nothing more than 'a vague willingness to suppose that "there's something out there"',[7] accompanied by 'an unsurprising disinclination' to spend time or effort worshipping whatever the something might be. Those subscribing to this view have coined the derogatory term 'fuzzy fidelity' to describe what they see as a casual loyalty to a religious tradition without commitment to its institutions – and a lack of authentic faith defined in terms of orthodox Christian beliefs.[8] However, the burden of empirical evidence demonstrates that an individual's ceasing regular engagement with a local church does not necessarily – or even usually – imply a loss of faith or intentional turning away from Christianity.

As mentioned in the previous chapter, the most extensive and meticulous research undertaken among church-leavers in England and Wales, the *Church Leaving Applied Research Project*, found that about two-thirds of church-leavers retain their Christian faith.[9] Michael Fanstone's book, *The sheep that got away*, reported

---

6. Bruce, S., 2002, *God is dead: Secularization in the West*, Oxford: Blackwell, p. 197.

7. Voas, D. and Crockett, A., 2005, 'Religion in Britain: Neither believing nor belonging', *Sociology*, 39(1), pp. 11–28, pp. 24–5.

8. Voas, D., 2009, 'The rise and fall of fuzzy fidelity in Europe', *European Sociological Review*, 25(2), pp. 155–68.

9. Richter and Francis, *Gone but not forgotten*.

that only 7 per cent of church-leavers of over 500 he surveyed pointed to 'God issues'[10] as their reason for leaving church.[11] This resonates with Alan Jamieson's work in New Zealand. He found that only one of the 108 people he interviewed left church with the intention of moving away from their Christian faith. Indeed, the others were clear that they were not choosing to leave the Christian faith when they left the church.[12]

My own research found that, in the north of Scotland, 44 per cent of a random sample of 2,698 members of the general public identified themselves as Christians who do not regularly attend a local church congregation. For many people, this finding prompts a number of questions: what did they mean by 'Christian'? Are these people using that term merely as a cultural label? Are they complicit in what researchers call 'social desirability bias', a genuine phenomenon by which people tend to respond to survey questions in the way that they think will make them look best in the eyes of the person conducting the survey? What do people mean by 'regular attendance' and what qualifies as a 'local church congregation'?

The risk of different understandings of the same terms is real. For this reason, the terminology used in this research was clearly defined and carefully explained. A 'Christian', in the context of this survey, was defined as someone who would identify themselves as having a personal faith in Jesus Christ and would say that they seek to live in line with his teaching and example. To enable comparison with other studies, a definition of 'regular attendance' used by previous researchers was adopted. It was explained to participants that this should be taken to mean attending a minimum of six congregational worship services (excluding weddings, funerals, Christmas and Easter) in a year. A 'local

---

10. This appears to include both loss of faith in this context and the development of a view of God which wasn't reflected in the church they left.

11. Fanstone, M. J., 1993, *The sheep that got away*, Oxford: Monarch.

12. Jamieson, *A churchless faith*, p. 42.

church congregation' was defined as a group of Christians who meet together regularly for worship and is part of a wider denomination or network. The word 'local' meant that 'internet church' was not included, but there was no geographical limit to what is considered 'local' so long as the 'regular attendance' criteria were fulfilled.

The risk of 'social desirability bias', that tendency for people to provide what they think might be the desired answer, was also taken seriously. Embedded within the survey was a set of ten questions, which, together, formed an index known as the Hoge Intrinsic Religiosity Scale (HIRS). This may sound like academic gobbledygook with no relevance to people's real experiences of faith. However, this set of questions has been used extensively in other research and found to give a reliable insight into the nature of a person's faith. Indeed, the eminent author of a review of various similar research tools recommends this one as 'by far the most accurate measure of what I think is at the heart of religious devotion – relationship with and commitment to God'.[13] The ten questions were spread throughout the survey and when the responses were analysed together they generated a score between ten and fifty. High scores on this scale indicate that a person's faith underpins all that they do; their faith is core to their motivation and, in this sense, they *live* their faith. Lower scores suggest that they perceive their faith as having less impact on their life. It would be inappropriate and incorrect to apply labels such as 'nominal', 'committed' or 'devout' to groups within the sample according to their scores on this scale. However, it is noticeable that high scorers (i.e. those with scores more than thirty) show significant differences in their responses to many of the other questions compared with 'low scorers'. Prayer and reading the Bible are significantly more important to

---

13. Koenig, H. G., 2011, *Spirituality and health research: Methods, measurements, statistics and resources*, West Conshohocken, PA: Templeton Foundation Press, p. 229.

them, for example; they are much more likely to talk about their faith with others.

So, now I've convinced you of the reliability of the study, what was discovered? Well, the survey found that of those 44 per cent of people who identified themselves as Christians who do not attend church on a regular basis, about half were 'high scorers', demonstrating that their faith is central to their life. In terms of the science and statistics involved, we can be 95 per cent confident that (within a range of ± 5 per cent) 22 per cent of the people in the research area have a Christian faith that is a prominent influence in their lives. Follow-up research in the rest of Scotland produced broadly similar results. This and other data unmasks as a myth the idea that people who claim to be Christians but not church-goers are not really either. Such an understanding is a misconception based on either a misreading of the evidence or prejudice.

And finally . . .

One person who commented on a draft of this chapter taught me a new word in the process. He suggested that I might be in danger of 'enantiodromia'. Having reached for the dictionary, I realised that he was referring to the tendency to replace one thing with its opposite. In this case, his concern was that I might replace one set of stereotypes and prejudices with a romanticised or rose-tinted picture of those who leave church. He has a point. In attempting to simplify complex data, I am guilty of 'generalising'. However, the observations I have shared reflect the *dominant* themes and patterns. They are based on sound evidence, but should not be taken as implying that other narratives are not present.

On behalf of the hundreds of 'churchless Christians' I have interviewed and surveyed, thank you for listening. Samuel heard God's voice and had the courage to set aside stereotypes and look beyond outward appearances. As we encounter the evidence of hard data and the personal stories of churchless Christians, may we be prepared, where necessary, to revise our understanding and amend our convictions. May we exchange anecdote for evidence-based actuality, supplant fallacy with fact, refute stereotypes and rejoice in the certainty that, whether church-goer or non-congregational believer, we, 'though many, are one body in Christ, and individually members one of another' (Romans 12:5, RSV).

So what?
Questions and activities
for further reflection

'In a complex world [stereotypes] provide a kind of shorthand, as we ascribe to individuals the characteristics of others whom we have met or, more often, heard about second-hand . . . or third-hand . . . or fourth-hand.' Consider for a moment the different areas of housing in your community. Do you have any preconceptions about 'the kind of people' who live in each? What about the people who attend different churches? And how about different generations? Pray, asking God to show you dimensions of people's characters of which you were previously unaware.

Are there other Christians who you find difficult for any reason? Bring them to mind, hold them before God in prayer as you recall that we 'are one body in Christ, and individually members one of another' (Romans 12:5, RSV).

Read again the first section of this chapter. Take hold of Chimamanda Ngozi Adichie's phrase, 'the danger of the single story' and ask God in prayer to help you to hear when people, groups of people and complex issues are being described in terms of a 'single story'. Pray for greater sensitivity to recognise this in your own thinking.

CHAPTER 4

Exit routes

These days we can trace the awe-inspiring travels of migrating birds and map the ocean wanderings of dolphins and whales. How bizarre, then, that we have made minimal effort to discover the routes by which a multitude of people have left churches. We know little about the lives of Christians whose journeys of faith take them beyond congregations or never lead them into congregations. Based on recent studies, this chapter explores the common elements of the road to post-congregational faith.

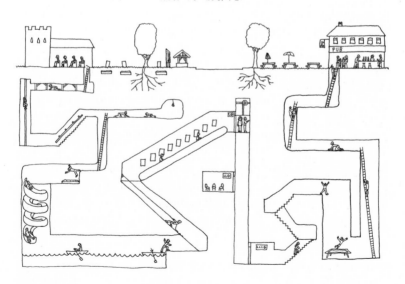

That same day two of Jesus' followers were walking to the
village of Emmaus, seven miles from Jerusalem. As they
walked along they were talking about everything that had
happened. As they talked and discussed these things, Jesus
himself suddenly came and began walking with them.

Luke 24:13–15

It was 'the first day of the week, very early in the morning'.[1] This
chapter of Luke's careful account begins at dawn on a day that
heralded the beginning of a new era. As the magnificent truth that
'he has risen!' gradually spreads among his followers, confusion
and despair are transformed into inexpressible joy. What a roller
coaster of emotional extremes Luke shares with us. First we meet
a group of grief-stricken women embarking on a sorrow-filled
labour of love. Taking spices to the tomb, they are bewildered to
find it empty. Then, hearing that everything has happened just as
Jesus had told them, they fall on their faces, awestruck and overcome with joy.

Just as our spirits soar with the women racing to share this
astonishing news, our excitement is dulled by the disbelief of the
disciples. And then we are taken to a dusty road where we meet
two travellers. They are dismayed, bruised by the excruciating
events of the previous days. They have heard the account of the
women, but clearly not believed it. Dispirited and disorientated,
they drag their feet along the road, away from the scene of what
they had thought to be life-changing encounters with Jesus, away
from his humiliation – and theirs, for they had staked their lives
on this man. As a fellow-traveller draws alongside we are given
an insight into the frame of mind of these two heartbroken disciples. It is summed up in their words, 'we had hoped'.[2] Events
had not played out as they had longed for. All indications had
been that Jesus was the one they had been waiting for, the long-
awaited liberator, the one who would break the shackles of Roman

---

1. Luke 24:1.
2. Luke 24:21.

occupation and herald a new age of peace and prosperity. But now he was dead and buried and, with him, their hope too.

Just as our spirits hit rock bottom, we get the first inklings of faith reawakening within the two weary and perplexed disciples. Like a guttering candle, so close to being extinguished, their hope flickers, recovers and then flames as Jesus, gently, graciously, unveils the glorious truth that he lives and that death has been swallowed up in victory. Just as their hope had been buried with him, so now it is resurrected with him. As they exited Jerusalem they had left behind long-nurtured dreams and precious hopes. They had turned their backs on what, just days before, had been a lifelong commitment. But now, out here on the highway, Jesus finds them once again, walks with them, teaches them, shares sustenance with them, leaves them with hearts aflame and a renewed pledge to follow him to the ends of the earth.

The controversial American comedian, Lenny Bruce, once quipped, 'Every day people are straying away from the church and going back to God.'[3] What was intended as satirical was in fact a word of truth. The fact that people are abandoning church has long been undeniable. However, what we now know is that a sizable majority of those who have exited congregations continue to see their Christian faith as central to their lives. For many, their departure from church is an expression of faith rather than a denial of it. Yes, there will be hurt and pain, but they are often driven in part by a hunch that only if they leave can their faith really flourish. Among those who leave church with their confidence in God in tatters, many find their faith kindled, even stoked.

Indeed, the encounter that Luke records on the road to Emmaus is an eloquent metaphor for the experience of many who have left churches. These congregations have, in the past, often been the context of much inspiration, encouragement, and, not least, friendship. Having moved away, people typically travel the road of bewilderment and grief, but then find that Jesus meets them afresh. *Why* people disengage from congregations will be explored

---

3. Retrieved 7 July 2015, from BrainyQuote.com website: www.brainy quote.com/quotes/quotes/l/lennybruce136592.html.

later. The focus of this chapter is the *how*. It is concerned with the *process* of disengagement, the inner and outer journeys that take people to the fringes of congregational life – and then beyond.

The dejected trek towards Emmaus of Cleopas and his friend was transformed into a profound pilgrimage by the presence of Jesus. Their faith was restored and their understanding deepened. As I have listened to Christians who have walked away from religious institutions or, in some cases, have never been part of a congregation, time and again I have heard that they too have discovered the truth of Jesus' promise, 'I will be with you always.'[4] As they have shared the road with others, they testify to the veracity of his claim that, 'where two or three gather in my name, there am I with them'.[5]

Along the way, especially when struggling at the fringes of congregational life and soon after disengagement, feelings of disappointment, loss, and confusion are commonplace. The actual decision to leave church is often marked by fear. As one church-leaver said, 'I think the "boundary" of the church is very much one of fear: "Maybe I will stop hearing God, maybe I am backsliding, maybe I am making a terrible mistake?"' However, with few exceptions, those I have listened to report arriving in a better place. What feels at times like a walk of shame or a march of misery and misunderstanding, becomes an adventure of faith. Without rotas and responsibilities, with identity no longer propped up by the scaffolding of organisational roles, a refocusing occurs.

The heartfelt yearning conveyed in those words 'we had hoped' expresses how many members of congregations feel about church. We crave a return to the glory days. We long for God to revive our congregations. On a personal level *we had hoped* that commitment to a local congregation would fuel our spiritual growth. *We had hoped* that the church would be effective in sharing the message of Jesus with our family and friends. *We had hoped* that our labours in the church would fulfil our sense of Christian vocation. For some, of course, these hopes are satisfied. But for

---

4. Matthew 28:20.
5. Matthew 18:20.

others there are experiences of disappointment and frustration. They love the people, but find that congregational infrastructure and duties take on a life of their own. The organisational minutiae of congregational life too easily become the focus of a disproportionate amount of attention, time and energy. The writer to the Hebrews knew the crucial importance and the surprising necessity of the reminder to 'Keep your focus on Jesus'.[6]

Whether you are wholeheartedly committed to a local congregation, struggling on the fringes, or a Christian with no congregational involvement, listening to, and learning from, those who are living a 'churchless faith' will both reassure and challenge.

Gradual but mindful

One matter about which there is widespread agreement between all the studies in relation to church-leaving is that, for most, disengagement from church is a gradual process over a prolonged period, usually several years. In my own research, about two-thirds of church-leavers agreed with the statement, 'I used to go to church but decreased attendance gradually over time.' Even those who stated that their departure was 'sudden' usually recognised that there were processes of withdrawal going on at a subconscious level long before they finally decided or recognised that they were leaving church.

While this finding concurs with data from England and Wales (Richter and Francis) and from New Zealand (Jamieson), there is an important contrast between my own findings and Jamieson's interpretation. Although he agrees that the 'vast majority of those who were interviewed did not leave their church suddenly',[7] he also states that many of his interviewees 'drifted' out of the church, often realising only in retrospection that they had left.[8] This idea of an unconscious drift out of church runs counter to the experiences

---

6. Hebrews 12:2.
7. Jamieson, A., 2002, *A churchless faith*, London: SPCK, p. 32.
8. Jamieson, A., *A churchless faith*, p. 32.

of church-leavers in Scotland. Those I have interviewed and surveyed talk of a more conscious process than Jamieson's interpretation would suggest. Rather than 'drifting' out of church, for most people it is an intensely mindful, conscious, thoughtful process. An accurate portrayal of the journey of church-leavers involves soul-searching, wrestling with guilt, and careful consideration. While disengagement may be accompanied with feelings of relief there are also experiences of loss and grief. The comment by one interviewee, 'I kind of feel guilty that I don't go to church any more' was similar to those of many who had disengaged relatively recently.

In time, such feelings fade and peace returns. So, someone who had left a congregation some years before presented a fairly typical report of life beyond the immediate anguish of disengagement, when she said:

I think the overwhelming experience is of a much better – I was going to say 'balance' but it's not all about balance – much better 'equilibrium' . . . there's a sense of being in the right place, doing the right things, which really helps [us], I think, to take the opportunities of the time and the talents and the gifts that we've been given and that is just a very strong impression of kind of where we stand today.

The road towards leaving a congregation is rarely travelled alone. Intertwined with their personal struggling and a growing sense of disquiet, most of those I have listened to also describe a process of communication with church leaders and friends. Sometimes this is reported as helpful. For others, some of the greatest angst and disappointment results from the disappointing response of others. Many church-leavers report a growing sense of not being understood. One interviewee outlined a five-year process of communication with church leaders: 'it took us probably a couple of years' thinking and then we put that [a letter explaining this couple's struggles with congregational life] together [and] presented it. And then there was a subsequent three years of discussion'. Another interviewee described attempts to discuss issues that were concerning him with his fellow Elders and the frustration with the lack of empathy or even response:

> Whenever I did try and sort of communicate and try and speak about problem situations that I felt were hard [and] were needing to be resolved, I just always felt as if it was – there was nothing came back. It was just like speaking – I always had a picture of speaking into a well and waiting for the echo but nothing came back at all. It was just – [I] felt quite unsupported and uncared for in situations that I was finding I was struggling with.

In seeking to understand the journey towards church-leaving it is necessary to recognise that, like strands woven together into a rope, at least three separate dynamics are tightly intertwined. First, the individual Christian is on a unique journey of personal development and spiritual growth, with its own seasons, peaks and troughs. Just over one in three of those surveyed in the *Investigating the Invisible Church*[9] study agreed with the statement 'Changes that happened within me led to me stopping attending church.' Second, the culture of a church congregation is a distinctive, multi-layered and changing context. And third, circumstances and events in and beyond the life of the individual and the congregation inevitably have important impacts. Stuff happens: new jobs and unemployment, broken relationships and new relationships, additional family members and bereavement, ill health and much more.

The ways in which congregations respond to the crises of life are crucial. The church's response can be instrumental in drawing people into greater commitment. It can also drive them towards, or beyond, the congregational fringes. Like rocks in the bed of a

---

9. *Investigating the Invisible Church* is available for free download here: www.resourcingmission.org.uk/sites/default/files/downloads/Investigating the invisible church.pdf. A more comprehensive account of this research was published in the peer-reviewed journal, *Rural Theology*: 'A Survey of Christians in the Highlands and Islands who are not part of a Church Congregation', *Rural Theology*, 12(2), November 2014, pp. 83–95.

stream, sometimes life's crises cause turbulence, but the general flow of life rolls on in the same overall direction. At other times these boulders take the flow in a whole new direction. For those already worn down by disappointment or frustration, crises and the response (or lack of response) within the congregation can be 'final straws', confirming niggling doubts regarding whether church is the place for them, and cementing decisions to disengage.

Mapping exit routes

In a typical one-liner, my favourite comedian, Tim Vine, declares: 'Exit signs [pause] – they're on the way out'. As we consider the process of disengagement from church, are there signs that mark the typical route taken? Having listened to the experiences of hundreds of church-leavers I am convinced that each person's journey is unique. However, I also recognise that, in studying and comparing interview transcripts and survey data, some well-worn paths emerge. A progression can be seen in the common journeys of church-leavers.

Although it is true to say that there is a typical series of experiences that lead from congregational life to something else, it would be wrong to suppose that the next steps are ever predictable by what has gone before. There are many people who experience seasons of disillusionment with their church, who lessen their commitment and involvement, but who do not then leave the congregation. Later they may renew their dedication and intensify their involvement – or they may continue to be affiliated but with diminished commitment. What can be said is that, based on a substantial body of evidence, it is possible to offer a model that takes seriously the complex realities of faith journeys, but expresses them in a simplified way.

If you are thinking that these kinds of 'model' are theoretical twaddle and of no practical use, your concern is understandable. Academic jargon can sometimes obscure real-world, down-to-earth application. The abstract form of some models can appear distant from the complex and sometimes painful realities they claim to represent. However, in the same way that we can helpfully explain the complexities of economics in terms of 'supply' and 'demand', so a simplified theory or model of the process of disengagement from church offers an important tool for those who want to understand.

For church leaders and concerned members of congregations such a model offers a means of enhanced understanding which can shape a pastoral response and inform congregational practices. To the church-leaver and those struggling to make sense of their all-too-real personal experiences of doubt, struggle and mounting frustration, a model can provide assurance that they are not alone, the encouragement that others have walked this way and survived, and a means of re-orientation and understanding their own predicament.

It is because of this conviction regarding the value and importance of such frameworks that I offer a simple model, a generalised 'road to post-congregational faith'. While unquestionably influenced by other frameworks (especially those related to bereavement,[10] disengagement[11] and deconversion[12]), this has developed from the careful analysis of the empirical evidence.

The road to post-congregational faith

The experiences of church-leavers rarely, if ever, form a tidy sequence. The reality is messy. Different stages overlap. However, there is a clear trajectory, and five distinct phases can be identified in most interviews with post-congregational Christians. They are phases which appear to be easily identified in retrospect by people who have travelled this road.

Although there may be overlap between phases, there is a definite order. One phase sometimes begins before another has reached its

---

10. Kübler-Ross, E., 1969, *On death and dying*, London: Routledge.

11. Ebaugh, H., 1988, Leaving Catholic convents: Toward a theory of disengagement, in Bromley, D., '*Falling from the faith: Causes and consequences of religious apostasy*, Newbury Park, CA: Sage, pp. 100–21.

12. Skonovd, L. N. J., 1979, *Becoming apostate: A model of religious defection*, cited in Richter, P. and Francis, L. J., 1998. *Gone but not forgotten: Church-leaving and returning*, London: Darton, Longman & Todd, p. 17.

culmination, but none are likely to begin in any substantive way before some progress is made in the previous phases. The five phases are as follows:

1. Asking questions and exploring doubts;
2. Cumulative disaffection;
3. Investigating, experimenting and evaluating;
4. Tipping points, 'final straws' and opportunities;
5. Detox, grief and moving on.

Asking questions and exploring doubts

It is tempting to think that wrestling with doubt arrived with the scepticism of the Enlightenment, the rationality of the scientific revolution, or the loss of certainty associated with postmodernism. However, the Hebrew Scriptures are peppered with cries that emanate from the agonies of doubt. Even when God's very existence is unquestioned, his presence, nature and care are often questioned. So, for example, we hear the heart-rending cry of David, echoed in the words of Jesus on the cross: 'My God, my God, why have you abandoned me? Why are you so far away when I groan for help?'[13]

Theologians and philosophers have long wrestled with the 'hiddenness' of God. His invisibility means that the life of faith is inevitably punctuated with questions and intermingled with doubt. Most of us can relate to the experience of American poet, Emily Dickinson, who wrote to a friend that she both believed and disbelieved a hundred times an hour and observed that this is what kept her faith 'nimble'.[14] Certainly her words find resonance within the accounts of many Christians who have ceased to be church-goers. They often speak of their need to ask questions and explore doubts – and their frustration or disappointment with churches which neither encourage nor facilitate these things. As one interviewee observed, 'Within most churches there

---

13. Psalm 22:1.

14. Johnson, T. H., 1958, *The letters of Emily Dickinson*, Cambridge, MA: Belknap, p. 728.

is little opportunity to talk openly about not only issues but also to openly share feelings about one's own faith.' Another felt that, 'If you do question, you're a renegade. Nobody's said that to me, but it was the feeling I got – that could be a wee touch of paranoia, but I don't think I'm wrong . . . Questioning isn't encouraged in many church contexts.'

Francis and Richter found similar evidence in their study in England and Wales and stressed the vital role that doubting and questioning plays in church-leaving. They found that many church-leavers felt that their local church neither welcomed nor wished to deal with people who doubted their faith. Of their sample of church-leavers, 16 per cent felt that nobody in their church would have understood their doubts, 25 per cent said that their church did not allow people to discuss or disagree with its views, and 29 per cent indicated that questioning faith did not seem acceptable to their church.[15]

It is a tragedy when churches treat doubt as an enemy. Like the father begging Jesus for the deliverance of his son, at some time or other most of us find ourselves crying, 'I do believe, but help me overcome my unbelief!'[16] The Christian's growth towards maturity involves a faith that coexists with doubt. Despite popular notions to the contrary, the opposite of doubt is not faith, but certainty – and certainty closes down all need of faith. Philip Yancey, never one to side-step the difficult issues, describes doubt as 'the skeleton in the closet of faith' and suggests that the constructive approach to confronting it is to bring it into the open and expose it for what it is. Doubt is neither to be concealed nor to be feared. Taking the 'skeleton in the closet' analogy a step further, Philip Yancey suggests that doubt too can provide the basis on which living matter may grow.[17]

When churches exclude room for doubt and for grappling with it, they fail to understand the nature of discipleship. When eager

---

15. Francis, L. J. and Richter, P., 2007, *Gone for good? Church-leaving and returning in the 21st century*, Peterborough: Epworth Press, p. 102.

16. Mark 9:24.

17. Yancey, P., 2000, *Reaching for the invisible God*, Grand Rapids, MI: Zondervan, p. 41.

disciples cannot find in church the space and companionship they need to explore questions and doubts, they seek these things elsewhere. For some this eventually leads to the abysmal and paradoxical choice between loyalty to a congregation and authenticity in their Christian spirituality.

Even with the support and understanding of a wise congregation, battles with doubt regarding the basics of the faith themselves require great courage, perseverance and humility. One interviewee, describing a lengthy and distressing tussle with doubt which led him away from church, recalled with a gravity born of emotional trauma:

> I'd lost something . . . and, over a period of years, I tried to be aware of what was happening and analyse it and it took me three years really to work out what was happening. But generally speaking I would say that I found that I could not accept a lot of the Christian premises of belief. I became even more disenchanted with the church and I felt that I could not really carry on as I was. During this time I found that because I had believed for so long, the whole of my life, I could not bring myself to comfortably think about questioning the Christian faith, let alone voicing it, and eventually I decided that I would tell my wife, and that was the first time that I vocalised it, which was quite hard . . . Anyway, once I was able to say that I was questioning what I believed, then that allowed me to investigate that more.

The role of doubt in Christian discipleship will be explored in greater depth in other chapters. For now, suffice it to say that individual believers and churches alike do well to recognise that encountering the 'dark night of the soul' and 'wilderness experiences' are integral to the Christian life. They are part of developing trust in the total faithfulness of God and unlearning to trust in our capacity to know, to be certain, and to eliminate doubt.

For some people, their burning questions and escalating doubts relate not to God and personal faith, but to a particular church congregation, denomination, or church institutions in general. When seeking prospective interviewees through articles in local newspapers I received considerable correspondence from people who, although still engaged with a congregation, were keen to tell me that these kinds of struggles meant that their commitment to church was becoming ever more tenuous. '[I'm] holding on by my fingernails' said one. '[I've got] one foot in the back door [of the church]'. One particularly impassioned response read:

> Anyway, I thought I might just let you know that, not only are there people out there who have 'Churchless Faith', but there are others who are seriously considering it – me for one! My faith is as strong as it's ever been (along with all the usual doubts etc.) but I am seriously wondering whether the [name of denomination], or indeed any other organised religion, is an appropriate or healthy place to express it . . . I love the [church], it won me over sixteen years ago with its love and power when I had barriers against organised religion a mile high – it smashed them down. Now, however, I feel myself going right back to square one.

Cumulative disaffection

In all the interviews and surveys I have conducted with church-leavers I have never yet come across a person who left a congregation after a single catastrophic incident. Rather, the usual pattern is similar to the cumulative effect of a medical treatment. In the world of medicine, a 'cumulative effect' describes the phenomenon by which repeated administration of a drug leads to outcomes that are more pronounced than those produced by the first dose. In a context where there are inadequate opportunities to ask questions, raise concerns and explore doubts, disaffection begins to accumulate and multiply. Unrealised hopes lead to disappointment. Unaddressed concerns produce frustration. Disenchantment with leadership develops. Disillusionment with church grows. Like a snowball growing and gathering momentum as it rolls downhill, a sense of estrangement increases and intensifies. This is 'cumulative disaffection'.

It would be a mistake to imagine that 'cumulative disaffection' is purely about church-leavers experiencing frustration and gradually distancing themselves. It is never a simple, one-sided development. 'Cumulative disaffection' is usually a mutual process. There is a kind of 'mutual withdrawal'.[18] In parallel with the church-leaver's growing sense of alienation, there is also a 'distancing' from them on the part of others within the congregation, especially those in leadership. This may be conscious, unconscious or sub-conscious. It may be in response to diminishing attendance or perceived criticism.

Whatever the reason, rather than reaching out to potential leavers, there is sometimes a stepping back by others in the congregation. Among those I have interviewed, one woman spoke of feeling 'kept at arm's length' after becoming less regular in her attendance at Sunday worship services. Another, a young man, felt 'left to drift' after sharing a concern with the minister of his congregation. It seems likely that this phenomenon of mutual retreat lies behind the finding in England and Wales that, in the case of 92 per cent of leavers, no-one from the church had talked with them about why they were attending less frequently during the weeks after their church-going declined or ceased.[19]

Investigating, experimenting and evaluating

Unsurprisingly, as disaffection takes root, people often begin to look beyond the congregation. They search for alternative opportunities for fellowship, worship and discipleship. For some this involves investigating other congregations and leads to them 'switching' rather than leaving congregational life altogether. However, those who become non-congregational Christians either fail to find a suitable congregation or, more often, have become disillusioned with the congregational way of being church.

An analogy used by one church-leaver I listened to provides a powerful image of how it feels to be on the brink of disengaging from a church congregation: 'The gap between the two trapezes is a scary place to be. Once you let go, there's no going back – for sure. But neither do you know if you are going to catch that other [trapeze].' That sense of not wanting to let go without having the other trapeze at least within sight is no doubt part of what

---

18. Ebaugh, 'Leaving Catholic convents'.
19. Francis and Richter, *Gone but not forgotten*, p. 145.

motivates those who are disaffected with church to explore alternatives. From the evidence of research in Scotland we know that this can take many forms. Some turn to the internet. Others recall finding books that assured them of a Christian life beyond the congregation. As one interviewee reflected:

> I've always been sustained by books and articles that have sort of spoken to me and I would have thought that was a sort of main element of sustenance, rather than sermons . . . Coming across stuff like *A churchless faith*[20] and re-reading Anne Townsend's book[21] and sort of realising it's actually OK to question.

Some of those I have listened to mentioned retreat centres, Christian communities and conferences as places of nurture and encouragement that they visited. Some described a realisation that, for them, 'the cathedral of God's creation' is where they came alive spiritually. One young man explained:

> From my point of view I don't go to church because I see more of God when I'm climbing the hills and kayaking the rivers, and I'm happy to meet people and we have some really good discussions . . . We've been to Christian things, but not church. We've been to conferences and I'm really into music, so I've been to hear different Christian bands play . . . .

For some the search for an alternative to the congregation they have been part of is intentional, like stretching out and reaching for that other trapeze. For others, they stumble upon resources, contacts or ideas which encourage them to step out of the congregation. Either way there is a process of evaluation, a weighing up of the relative merits of staying put or moving on. This often includes discussions with spouse, friends or respected others. A non-judgemental, listening ear and wise counsel within the

---

20. Jamieson, *A churchless faith*.
21. This person was referring to the book *Faith without pretending* by Anne J. Townsend, 1990, London: Hodder & Stoughton.

congregation is a godsend. However, it is not unusual to encounter defensiveness, misunderstanding or denial. One man, an Elder in a congregation for many years, described the unwillingness of people to hear about the crisis he was going through:

> I'd certainly discussed it with the minister there, and a couple of close friends within the church. The friends, to be honest, couldn't really come to terms with it and couldn't understand it, so it's not that I didn't get support from them but, having told them, they almost didn't want to know. In other words, 'don't tell me any more', and even when I decided I was resigning from the Eldership I told certain friends, 'Look, please, this is not a secret – if anyone is puzzled as to what is happening here, then do tell them, in your own words, what you understand by what's happened here about me', but they were reluctant to do that. Funnily enough when I did resign, hardly anyone asked me, hardly anyone.

Tipping points, 'final straws' and opportunities

Already drained by the chronic frustrations and disappointments and after a period of contemplating leaving church, other issues often intervene. In some cases, the issues are from within the church and become the proverbial 'straw that breaks the camel's back'. For example, one married couple who had long been exasperated by poor communication in their congregation decided to leave after one particularly infuriating incident. In their case, the minister made a unilateral and unexpected decision to end an activity that had been precious to them for a considerable time and in which they had invested a lot of energy:

> He decided to close the Bible study down without coming and speaking to us or asking us or saying, 'Look, I'm going to do something different'. He just announced from the pulpit that next week will be the last one and then it'll be closed.

Sometimes the incident that becomes the tipping point is unrelated to church. Typical examples are marriage breakdown, health problems and financial difficulties. In the *Investigating the invisible church* study, just over a fifth of respondents (21 per cent) said that this sort of crisis in their life led to them disengaging from church. The proportion of those who had previously attended church for more than twenty years who pointed to this kind of crisis leading them away from church was particularly high (33 per cent). So, at the very times when we might expect to find people drawing practical and emotional support from the congregation they belong to, we see that some move away. This is probably explained at least in part by responses to another question in the same survey, as a fifth of respondents stated that they had felt 'let down by the church at a time of personal need'.

Once we ascertain that most people leave congregations gradually, the role of tipping points and 'final straws' is predictable. However, you may be more surprised at the word 'opportunities' above. This refers to the fact that, for some, the catalyst for departure is neither one final frustration from within the congregation nor one of the calamities that punctuate every life. Rather, it is a set of circumstances that allow a person to leave with minimal fuss. In some cases it may be that a situation presents itself where a person might leave 'with good reason'. One interviewee, for example, confessed that, after about three years of contemplating leaving the congregation, her mother's illness presented just such an opportunity:

> At this time my mother was living in [a town 100 miles away], in a home (she had dementia) – and I almost took it on myself to spend time with her on Sunday . . . I think the general understanding within the church was that because of my involvement and time that I was spending with my mother, that that somehow meant that I didn't have time to give my energies to the church.

While not usually viewed as a 'crisis', moving house is a time of considerable upheaval and is another common time for church-leaving. In my own studies, about one in six (17 per cent) agreed with the statement, 'I used to go to church but when I moved house I did not find a church I liked in my new area.' Interestingly, there was no difference in responses to this statement between those indicating higher or lower levels of commitment to the Christian faith.

Detox, grief and moving on

Detox? From church? You may feel that I have crossed a certain line in using such language. The Oxford English Dictionary defines detox as a 'process or period of time in which one abstains from or rids the body of toxic or unhealthy substances'. Now I would not suggest for a moment that most congregations are toxic or unhealthy places to be. Yes, there *are* toxic churches – congregations where relationships have totally broken down and where the qualities that characterise Christian community, such as love, joy and forgiveness, are heart-breakingly absent. However, in my experience at least, these are relatively rare.

Most congregations are contexts in which many of those associated with them are blessed through the experience. They are institutions that make positive contributions to their communities. However they are human institutions and therefore, inevitably, flawed. Some may point out that churches are more than human institutions – and they are correct. However, while they may be *more* than human organisations, they are never less. They are, therefore, vulnerable to all manner of mistakes and misunderstandings, susceptible to all kinds of error and omission. So, while it would be wrong to suggest that congregations are often toxic, it is also true that even the healthiest churches have potential to hurt and harm, to create an unhelpful environment for some people.

For most church-leavers there are two elements to detox. First it is necessary to recover from the emotional exhaustion or injury that has taken place. For some this will be a long, hard road. An article in the journal of the British Association for Behavioural and Cognitive Therapies in 2011 argued for wider recognition for 'Religious Trauma Syndrome'.[22] The author, Marlene Winell, bases her proposition on over twenty years of helping people

---

22. Winell, M., 2011, 'Religious trauma syndrome', *Cognitive Behaviour Therapy Today*, 39(4), pp. 19–21.

whose lives have been devastated by their experience of organised religion. She believes that there is an urgent need for mental health professionals to recognise the seriousness of Religious Trauma Syndrome. Winell reports that most of her cases are people who have suffered at the hands of churches that require 'rigid conformity' in order to continue in the congregation. She explains that as well as demanding strict adherence to certain principles and practices, these churches tend to use a closed system of logic and a strong social structure to support an 'authoritarian worldview'.

While this does not describe most churches, it is important to recognise that people who leave *any* church undertake a demanding transition. For most people, change is experienced as a loss before it is experienced as a gain. A grief reaction is triggered when people leave church. Grief is the natural reaction to loss and, even in the case of people who have been eager to leave church for some considerable time, there is still loss on multiple levels. While grief is a normal and a universal experience, it is also personal. Experts recognise typical 'stages of grief', but also acknowledge that every experience of grief is unique, personal and unpredictable.

Over the last three years I have collected dozens of testimonies from people who are detoxing from church. The internet abounds with blog posts from 'recovering Christians'. One blog entitled 'Why Church Detoxing Takes So Much Time' details a painful seven-year journey of recuperation and concludes that 'detoxing Christians' and those 'recovering after being church-damaged' usually need considerable time to process all that is has happened and allow emotional wounds to heal.[23]

The second aspect of detox is equally challenging, but also exciting and positive. For many church-leavers, participating in various meetings and being a Christian have become indistinguishably intertwined. In many congregations the Christian faith is 'parcelled and delivered' to its members, pre-digested by those in leadership. As will be explored in a later chapter, spiritual formation, discipleship, growing into ever greater Christ-likeness, is a blind spot for many congregations. It is integral to the Great Commission yet is

---

23. www.convergentbooks.com/why-church-detoxing-takes-so-much-time/.

so neglected that it has been dubbed the 'Great Omission'.[24] Most congregations are well aware of Jesus' command to 'Go into all the world and preach the Good News to everyone',[25] but place little emphasis on the call to 'make disciples . . . teach these new disciples to obey all the commands I have given you.'[26]

A result of this neglect is that those who go on to disengage from congregational life often need to learn or re-learn how to cultivate and live out their faith. One church-leaver I listened to expressed how, after many years of 'being spoon-fed [in a congregation] where Christianity was pre-packaged for me' he came to the realisation that all the activity of church had become for him 'this smokescreen that obscured the genuine state of my heart'. Dallas Willard, the influential writer on Christian discipleship, states that any effective process of spiritual formation will be remarkably similar to the Twelve-step programme practised by Alcoholics Anonymous groups all over the world.[27] Part of the success of this process is that it moves beyond detox to 'learning to live a new life with a new code of behaviour'.[28] For church-leavers who retain their faith, the focus of this book, there will be a process of re-formation as they discover and embed new ways of developing and practising their faith. We will explore some of these new ways in the chapters that follow.

---

24. Willard, D., 2006, *The great omission: Reclaiming Jesus's essential teachings on discipleship*, San Francisco, CA: HarperOne.

25. Mark 16:15.

26. Matthew 28:19–20.

27. Willard, D., 2002, *Renovation of the heart: Putting on the character of Christ*, Carol Stream, IL: Navpress, p. 85.

28. Heanue, K. and Lawton, C., 2012, *Working with substance users*, Maidenhead: McGraw-Hill Education, p. 60.

So what?
Questions and activities
for further reflection

How does the proposed model of 'The road to post-congregational faith' compare with your own experiences? If you have friends who are 'post-congregational Christians', ask them how it relates to their own journey.

The concept of 'mutual withdrawal' is introduced in this chapter: 'In parallel with the church-leaver's growing sense of alienation, there is also a distancing from them on the part of others within the congregation, especially those in leadership. This may be conscious, unconscious or sub-conscious. It may be in response to diminishing attendance or perceived criticism.' Does this help to make sense of any experience you have had? How does an awareness of this process enable you to counter its effect in your own relationships?

Are you aware of opportunities for 'asking questions and exploring doubts' in a non-threatening, non-judging context? Could you give anyone an opportunity to air questions and doubts?

What does the word 'doubt' mean to you? Is it an enemy to be fears or an invitation to grow or something else?

CHAPTER 5

A longing for belonging

From ancient wisdom to cutting-edge neuroscience, a sense of belonging is recognised as essential for a person's well-being. However, evidence indicates that even a church that is perceived as welcoming by many of its members can sometimes be the scene of 'unintentional exclusion'. This chapter looks at some of the wonderful ways in which we differ. It then explores how processes can exacerbate over-representation of certain groups, inadvertently creating a culture that is helpful and comfortable for some people, but challenging for others.

AFTER-SERVICE COFFEE

THIS IS THE TIME WHEN NEWCOMERS CAN GET TO KNOW THE CONGREGATION

Jesus, worn out by the trip, sat down at the well. It was noon. A
woman, a Samaritan, came to draw water. Jesus said,
Would you give me a drink of water? . . . The Samaritan
woman, taken aback, asked, How come you, a Jew, are ask-
ing me, a Samaritan woman, for a drink? (Jews in those
days wouldn't be caught dead talking to Samaritans.)

John 4:6–9 (MSG)

As a teenager I sometimes helped a friend and his father to move pigs from one area of the farm to another. The pigs were usually enclosed by a thin strand of electric fence. This was barely visible to the pigs, but if they made contact with that wire they got a painful shock. It was highly effective at keeping pigs in their proper place, but when the time to move them arrived and part of the fence was removed, it was almost impossible to coax them over the invisible line where the fence had been. Experience had taught them: don't challenge the boundaries!

The times and places in which the events of the New Testament occurred were characterised by complex systems of social barriers, fences designed to keep similar people together and different people apart. Like the electric fences at the pig farm, they were invisible to the untrained eye, but extremely effective. A severe jolt awaited anyone who dared to challenge them. Social conventions and religious laws established unyielding boundaries on the basis of belief, ethnic background, gender and other differences. They were particularly keenly applied between Jews and Samaritans. In fact, it was said by the Rabbis that to eat the bread of a Samaritan was like tucking into pork, something unimaginably repellent to a Jew.

We all see the world from where we stand and, from a Jewish point of view, mingling with Samaritans was bad, very bad. Imagine then, at a time when some Rabbis were forbidden to greet any woman, even their wife or daughter, in public, how a conversation with a *Samaritan woman* was regarded. It was scandalous, inexcusable. Not, however, in the eyes of Jesus. As if to underline the point, his interaction with this particular Samaritan woman was even more shocking. The fact that she needed to leave town in the searing heat of the midday sun in order to draw water, rather than in the morning with the rest of the women, was because of her disreputable history (v. 18). Jesus met her on her daily walk of shame.

Throughout the Gospels we find Jesus ignoring community expectations, challenging social convention, and subverting religious regulations. He treated differences with indifference. His was a ministry of radical inclusion. He understood that belonging, that sense of being included, is a basic human necessity. Just as air, light, warmth and water are vital if a plant is to thrive, so people have an indispensable need to belong. It's not a 'nice-to-have'; it's a 'must-have'. While not essential for life itself, psychologists are clear that the experience of belonging is crucial for healthy living. Its absence is linked to increased health problems, depression and even suicide.[1]

From ancient wisdom to cutting-edge neuroscience, the essential nature of belonging is acknowledged. People of all eras have known the truth that scientists now confirm: human beings are profoundly and universally motivated by a need to belong.[2] And yet, in Western cultures especially, we also have a deep-rooted inclination for independence. We long to belong, but we also like to maintain social distance and keep people at arm's length. The Fall of humankind expressed in the first chapters of Genesis not only led to estrangement between people and their Creator. It also resulted in broken relationships within his creation too – between people, and between them and their environment. The meta-narrative of the scriptures is that God has been striving to liberate his creation from alienation and decay ever since.

In the final book of the New Testament, John tries to describe the awe-inspiring glimpse he had been given of how things will be when God's ultimate intention is finally fulfilled. The scene he

---

1. The link between suicide and a lack of belongingness was proposed over a century ago (1897) in Émile Durkheim's seminal book, *Suicide*. The American journal, *Suicide and Life-Threatening Behavior*, has carried several papers in recent decades that add credibility to his original theory.

2. Baumeister, R. F. and Leary, M. R., 1995, 'The need to belong: Desire for interpersonal attachments as a fundamental human motivation', *Psychological Bulletin*, 117(3), pp. 497–529.

saw contained a multitude comprising people 'from every nation and tribe and people and language' (Revelation 7:9). Along with this exquisite variety, their common purpose was unmistakeable. Their gaze was fixed on a throne. Their attention was focused on 'the Lamb', Jesus Christ in his full glory. In John's Revelation we are presented with an image of diversity and unity in absolute harmony.

The extent to which individual church congregations are intended to be a foretaste of John's vision of diversity and unity is a subject of debate. Certainly, Christian community is to be a sign of God's final intention, a tantalising preview. However, bizarrely, we find that congregations seem to thrive and grow most when they are made up of similar people. Specialists in church growth call this the 'Homogenous Unit Principle'[3] and encourage the development of congregations that comprise people of a particular generation, interest group, ethnicity or other significant similarity. It may seem contradictory that a concept so apparently alien to the principles of Christian community expounded in the New Testament should 'work'. However, the empirical evidence demonstrates that it does. What are we to make of this? What did Paul have in mind when he wrote to Christian communities in Galatia: 'There is no longer Jew or Gentile, slave or free, male and female. For you are all one in Christ Jesus' (Gal. 3:28)?

If we remember that there is only one Church, the one, holy, catholic and apostolic Church of the creed, and that local church congregations are a minuscule part of that whole, perhaps it is

---

3. The HUP was proposed by Donald McGavran in his 1970 book, *Understanding church growth*. He suggested that for maximum impact people need to see the Christian faith lived out within their own culture. He therefore enjoined churches to appeal to people of similar language, ethnicity, generation etc. He has been criticised for pandering to consumerism rather than promoting a Kingdom worldview which breaks down barriers between people. Despite his critics, there has been increasing recognition in recent years of other theological themes which support the Homogeneous Unit Principle (see www.freshexpressions.org.uk/guide/about/principles/diversity/homogeneous).

easier to see that there is room for 'homogenous units'. John saw in his Revelation that distinct human cultures will be visible in eternity. It seems that there is no divine intention to achieve unity by subsuming everyone into a monochrome whole. Rather, unity will be expressed as people and groups of people, with their plethora of differences, are one with each other. There is no requirement for every local congregation to please everyone. Unity and mutual understanding are vital and need to be actively fostered, but it's OK for 'birds of a feather flock together'.

Expressing Christian community in assorted ways and preserving unity within the wider church is a challenge. Too often new Christian initiatives, seeking to engage with a particular group or culture, are seen as 'schisms' rather than 'green shoots', factions rather than examples of the multi-hued variety in which God seems to delight. In recent years the Fresh Expressions movement in the UK[4] has recognised the need for new congregations for people who share some particular sub-culture and has resulted in remarkable numerical growth.[5] Many people who had left church have been finding a community where they feel they belong and

---

4. www.freshexpressions.org.uk A fresh expression of church is a new gathering or network that engages mainly with people who have never been to church. There is no single model, but the emphasis is on starting something that is appropriate to its context, rather than cloning something that works elsewhere. Over 3,000 of these new forms of church now exist in almost every denomination and tradition in the UK. They seek to serve those outside church, listen to people and enter their culture, make discipleship a priority and form church.

5. Church of England Church Growth Research Programme, 2014, *From anecdote to evidence: Findings of the Church Growth Research Programme 2011–2013*, London: Church of England Archbishops' Council. Church congregations that grow tend to do so at the expense of other neighbouring congregations. However, a study of over 500 Fresh Expressions found that nearly half of the people who have engaged with these communities had not previously attended church. In addition, about a third of people in Fresh Expressions had been church-goers previously, but not recently. Indeed, overall it was found that for every one person that an existing congregation had released to begin a Fresh Expression of church, 2.6 people who were not previous church-goers joined these forms of Christian community.

can thrive. It is vital that we recognise and celebrate difference. If for no other reason, then simply because God does!

Unintentional exclusion

These reflections are important because one of the most common findings among Christians who are not engaged with a congregation is that they felt they did not belong in church. In the *Faith journeys beyond the congregations* study, more than a third of interviewees spoke of feeling that they could not 'be themselves'. Some used the term 'authenticity'. Others spoke of 'lacking a sense of belonging'. Factors included things as diverse as dress code, leadership structures, the role of women, expectations regarding spiritual experiences and more. Hear the voices of some of those I have listened to:

This is a problem that I tend to have with churches is that they tell you how you should be and they don't allow you to be authentic.

I couldn't conform to that sort of system.

For me to go to a church where you have to wear shirt and tie . . . if I don't wear a shirt and tie to the church they say to you 'You're not tidy enough. You're wearing a hooded top.' I'm not sure that's good and I find that difficult . . . I think God's much bigger than that.

I found it difficult to have the experiences that I thought other people had, and therefore I felt very much on the outside and unable to get on the inside.

Some simply found the congregation a difficult place to make friends, other than at a superficial level:

But that's what I wanted in the church – I wanted friends in the church, I didn't want a Sunday stranger.

I felt like I would walk in there on a Sunday morning and no-one was talking to me and I'd get on with doing my thing and the service would finish and we'd go out and could have absolutely no-one speak to me, and . . . that's nothing against them, because I think sometimes that happens in all sorts of places, but to think about church to me is to be in a loving family.

Speaking of his wife, one man explained that 'because of the role of women [in a particular denomination] she didn't feel welcomed . . . she felt like an addendum to me, kind of thing'.

A few of those interviewed explained how they sensed that some people were appreciated more than others and found themselves among those perceived to be less valued:

I struggled with the way some members of the church were valued more than others. That's what it always felt like – that older people weren't valued as much as the couples with families.

As this issue of belonging and inclusion emerged from the interviews as such a prominent theme, the *Investigating the invisible church* survey included three questions which probed whether part of the reason for disengaging from church was the lack of a 'sense of belonging'. The responses to these questions were remarkably similar across the board. Regardless of age, previous experience of church, score on the Hoge scale (see Chapter 3), and gender, about a quarter agreed with the statement, 'I used to go to church but felt that I didn't fit in.'

However, this lack of 'belongingness' in local congregations does not translate into a sense of alienation from the wider Church. Half of respondents indicated that they felt part of the worldwide Christian community. Only a fifth disagreed with the statement, 'I feel part of the worldwide Christian community.' However, this is a statement to which some groups responded in ways notably different from what the overall picture might suggest. Unsurprisingly, of those with higher than average scores on the Hoge scale a significantly higher proportion agreed with this statement (66 per cent) compared with those who scored less than average – of whom only 34 per cent agreed. Also, nearly two-thirds of respondents who had attended church for over twenty years (64 per cent) agreed with this statement compared with fewer than half of all those respondents who had attended for less time (45 per cent).

In the 2015 *Faith in Scotland* study, 815 people who identified themselves as 'Christian but not attending church' were asked the question, 'What would you say are the main reasons for you not attending church at the current time?' Once again, the issue of belonging and inclusion was prominent. Here are some representative responses:

Church is about community, but there is no community feel. I've been to many churches and don't feel this.

Where we live they are not very friendly.

It is difficult. We are from South Africa. They are more friendly and more welcoming [there] . . . If I was there, I wouldn't be known as 'the lady from South Africa'.

The nearest one is not for us. It is all blacks. I don't fit in.

They are not open minded enough to accept people from other races and cultures. I am from the Caribbean.

Whenever I do go to church, there's no-one the same age as me. It's nice speaking to people and meeting people, but it would be nice to meet people of the same age and the same interests. It would be refreshing.

Not mixing well with the people already in the church group. Nobody says anything to us.

Dare I say, 'holy huddles'? Little groups get together and if you go past them they speak about you.

All of this accords with the findings of studies in other parts of the UK and elsewhere. The first serious study of church-leaving in the USA found that the most often stated reason for leaving was a 'failure to feel that they were accepted, loved or wanted'.[6] Reflecting on the data of the *Church Leaving Applied Research Project*, Francis and Richter found that issues related to social exclusion played a significant part in the process of disengagement for nearly half of church-leavers.[7] Forty-five per cent of their sample indicated that they felt they did not belong. Twenty-five per cent said that there were cliques or 'in groups' from which they felt excluded. Twenty-two per cent specifically mentioned a lack of people of their own age group as an important factor.

Welcome or inclusion

Hearing the voices of some of the people quoted above could leave one with the impression that congregations are cold, unwelcoming assemblies of unfriendly people who gather to join in worshipping together in anonymity. No doubt there are churches where this is a reasonable description. However, having visited and worked with many dozens of congregations, I believe that by far the majority comprise people who earnestly want to extend a warm and heartfelt welcome. The signboard outside many churches states that 'All are welcome' and it is usually sincere in its intention.

Over recent years, along with other development workers in the Church of Scotland, I have facilitated *Entertaining angels* workshops for many churches, aimed at reviewing and improving the welcome they offer. I have often been impressed by the careful consideration that has already been given to expressing the fact that they are genuinely pleased to see new faces.

---

6. Hartman, W. J., 1976, *Membership trends: A study of decline and growth in the United Methodist Church 1949–1975*, Nashville, TN: Discipleship Resources, p. 40.

7. Francis, L. J. and Richter, P., 2007, *Gone for good? Church-leaving and returning in the 21st century*, Peterborough: Epworth Press.

The title of those workshops comes from that intriguing verse in the Letter to the Hebrews in which we are reminded to 'show hospitality to strangers, for some who have done this have entertained angels without realising it!'[8] That word translated as 'hospitality' (or 'welcome' in some versions) literally means 'the love of strangers (or outsiders)'. Hospitality, welcome and inclusion are important themes throughout the scriptures. The New Testament reserves some of its warmest commendation for those who are exemplary in their hospitality – and some of its sternest condemnation for those who refused to be 'lovers of strangers'.[9] In his letter to Titus, Paul declares that Christian leaders are to be 'lovers of hospitality'.[10] So, a paraphrase would be that leaders are to *love the love of outsiders*. Paul reminds followers of Jesus Christ in Rome to 'be *eager* to practice hospitality'.[11] This expresses the proactive dimension to the hospitality that is commended in the New Testament. At a time when 'hospitality' is an 'industry' and fear of strangers is often encouraged, these and other scriptures pronounce a prophetic word: love the outsider, the stranger.

Here, then, is an enigma. The Church's foundational text is clear that radical hospitality is a standard trait of genuine Christian community, many congregations are eager to be welcoming and yet there are many people who feel excluded. So what is going on? How can this be? Clearly a generous welcome from the perspective of some people does not necessarily equate to an experience of belonging and inclusion by others.

Is there evidence that helps us to resolve this conundrum? Are there findings from some of the research we have been exploring that will shed light on the processes at work? Are there insights to be gained that might enable Christians to avoid unintentional exclusion and to build relationships that both embrace diversity and pursue unity? The answer to these questions is 'yes'. But first

---

8. Hebrews 13:2.

9. In 3 John, for example, we find that Gaius is applauded for his hospitality – in contrast with Diotrephes who, 'refuses to welcome other believers'.

10. Titus 1:8.

11. Romans 12:13.

we need to do a little preparatory ground work. Before attempting to understand the processes that lead to alienation and exclusion, we need to understand some of the fundamental differences between individuals which influence their ability to engage with a church congregation.

The wonder-filled world of human difference

As we begin to think about some of the wealth of diversity that seems to so delight our Creator, it's time for a quick experiment. Please take a moment to consider this question: If you buy a new piece of computer software or an unfamiliar electrical gadget, how do you prefer to get to grips with it? Are you a person who likes to read the instruction manual first? Or would you rather just launch in, 'play around' and work things out for yourself? Or are you perhaps someone who would prefer to get some help, either by receiving some training or by inviting a more knowledgeable friend to assist? When speaking to groups of people about the growth of churchless faith, I have often asked people these questions. In every group, each of these preferences has been represented, often in almost equal number.

Educationalists tell us that, in any group of people, there will be a number of different preferred learning styles. Of course people are flexible to a degree. Most of us can act against our preferences without any great problem. However, if we are required to do so frequently and there are few opportunities that fit with our natural inclinations, then we are likely to become discouraged, frustrated or even distressed.

When we start to think about individual inclinations and personal preferences, we soon realise that there are *countless* variations. Surely, even to begin to consider them is a futile task. The question of preferred learning style mentioned above highlights just one of an incalculable array of differences that make up the wonderful, delightful variety of humanity.

While sitting in a local café recently to write this book, pondering this very matter, I was distracted by two women who bustled in with a gaggle of energetic toddlers. Sitting at a table by the window, one of the young mums drew the youngsters' attention to a small dog that was tethered outside: 'Look at the puppy. Do you think it's a little boy or a little girl?' 'NO!' one of the children cried, 'It's a dog.' He was right! It was neither boy nor girl. It was indeed a dog. The penny dropped: some differences are more important than others!

When it comes to finding a sense of belonging, an environment in which one feels unthreatened, unembarrassed and able to be authentically oneself without pretence, there are some differences that are instrumental and others that are inconsequential. Time and again data related to Christian faith and church-going shows that how congregations respond to differences of gender, generation, personality and marital status are especially important with regard to people experiencing (or not experiencing) a sense of belonging. You may be surprised by factors that are not in this list. Cleary there are a number of other aspects of personal difference that are of the *utmost* importance to certain people. Sexuality and theological persuasion are obvious examples. The truth is, however, that while matters other than gender, generation, personality and marital status are often cited as key motivations for church splits and frequently make media headlines, they do not emerge from the current research as issues of the same magnitude as the aforementioned factors.

So let's now explore the areas of personal difference that seem to most affect belonging in the context of churches – before attempting to explain some of the dynamics that shape the culture of churches and lead (or keep) people away from congregations.

Gender

Once upon a time Martians and Venusians fell in love. They respected and accepted their differences. Then they came to earth and they forgot they were from different planets. Don't worry, you haven't picked up the wrong book by mistake! This is the allegory that Dr John Gray uses in his book, *Men are from Mars, women are from Venus*.[12] Gray uses the metaphor of different planets to explain how many misunderstandings and relationship difficulties between men and women are rooted in fundamental differences between the genders. Since its publication in the early 1990s, very few non-fiction titles have sold more copies.

Every few years the media grasps a new piece of research which appears to confirm that traditional perceptions of gender originate from genuine neurological differences. In 2013, a minor media frenzy reported findings from the University of Pennsylvania, which demonstrated through the latest brain scanning techniques that women's brains are highly connected across the left and right hemispheres, whereas men's brains are characterised by strong connections between the frontal and rear areas. This, the researchers claimed, showed that men's brains are hardwired for perception and co-ordinated actions, and women's for social skills and memory. However, in the weeks that followed, scientists were quick to point out that, although the scans showed differences between the average brain of adult males and females, they did not begin to address the central concern of gender difference. Were the differences there since birth or the result of exposure to gender roles and stereotypes?

While the debate about the origin of gender has been going on, there have been substantial strides towards greater gender equality, both in the UK and globally. The idea that no-one should be discriminated against on the basis of gender is central the UN Universal Declaration of Human Rights. There is still much to be done, but considerable progress has been made in ensuring impartiality in law, employment and social situations. However, equality should not be confused with sameness. As well as the obvious biological differences between male and female, there are undeniable, observable differences in behaviour between genders. Whatever the origins and shapers of these differences, they are visible in most social contexts – and they are clearly detected in matters of faith and church.

---

12. Gray, J., 1993, *Men are from Mars, women are from Venus*, New York City, NY: HarperCollins.

On the whole, church congregations in the UK tend to have more women than men. Despite the fact that the numbers of women attending church have been falling more quickly than men in recent years,[13] the overall church-going population is still skewed towards women. The ratio of women to men is in the region of 60:40. When it comes to Christians who do not attend a church congregation, the evidence is somewhat contradictory. In my own studies in Scotland, the ratio of women to men among this group varied very little between regions and was always in the range 60:40 – 66:34. However, 2014 research carried out by YouGov on behalf of Christian Vision for Men and Single Christians Ltd, found that 10.5 per cent of people identified themselves as 'practising Christians but not attending a place of worship at least once a year' and that this represented slightly more men than women.[14] This is quite a marked difference, probably resulting from different definitions and different methodology. YouGov use an invited panel of internet users for their surveys and then weighted the responses in line with demographic information. The surveys in Scotland recruited a random sample by telephone.

Personality/psychological type

One approach to understanding personality uses psychometric testing, whereby questionnaires are used to measure psychological preferences. It evaluates how people make decisions and perceive the world. Perhaps the best-known example is the Myers–Briggs Type Indicator (MBTI). This assesses the psychological preferences of people with regard to four pairs of opposites and then

---

13. The numbers of women attending church have been falling more quickly than numbers of men, both in real and percentage terms, for some time. Overall, church congregations have become more male. In Scotland, for example, men made up 37 per cent of the church-going population in 1984, 39 per cent in 1994, and 40 per cent in 2002.

14. www.singlechristians.co.uk/info/yougov_report, p. 15.

assigns to an individual one of sixteen different 'psychological types'. So, for example, one pair of psychological preferences is introvert and extrovert. People who prefer extroversion are energised by action. They prefer to act and then reflect; they prefer *frequent* interaction with others. When extroverts are inactive, their motivation declines. Those whose preference is introversion tend to reflect and then act. For them, activity requires energy to be expended. To replenish their energy, introverts require quiet time alone. In engaging with other people they prefer *substantial* rather than frequent interaction.

One participant in the *Faith journeys beyond the congregations* study explained:

Obviously I am an introvert and I do not draw energy from being with others. In fact being with others drains me and I do not think that enough thought is taken of that in the way churches traditionally have operated – and I think that's quite an important thing.

Another interviewee proclaimed herself strongly extroverted and expressed the annoyance she felt because of the lack of interactive opportunities within congregations:

My Dad used to say, 'When I became a Christian I wanted nothing more than to sit at the feet of these Elders who had so much to say, so much wisdom that I need to learn from. Why can't you be like that?' For me, my main way of learning has been bouncing things around, throwing things around in conversation and in discussion, trying things out and seeing what happens . . . I used to find that by the end of a Sunday service I was bursting with questions. I needed to talk, but there was no chance. Even over coffee afterwards people were more interested to talk about the weather than what we had all just sat through.

No one psychological type is better or worse. They are just different. Rather like left-handedness and right-handedness, psychological types reflect preferences. For some these will be strong; others may feel that they occupy the middle ground. As Christians we can see in this rich variety the fingerprints of our Creator. God delights in diversity. Personality, psychological type, inevitably influences how our beliefs and spirituality are developed. People of different personalities warm to different aspects of the Christian story; they find different ways of expressing spirituality more or less helpful. Crucially, they find different styles of church helpful and fulfilling. Being forced into practices that grate with one's personality will be a cause of mild irritation for some and the root of severe anguish for others.

Age/generation

Just as different personalities, gender and the various ways in which people prefer to learn will shape how the Christian faith and church are experienced, so too *age* will influence how these are perceived and the kinds of practices that are found helpful. Some of the differences that are associated with age are easily noticeable. For example, the cognitive and physical abilities of humans develop – and then decline – with age. So the limited capacities of young children to understand complex concepts and the physical constraints on some elderly people are evident. Other age-related differences are less obvious, but nonetheless powerful in their influence on how we experience faith, church and, indeed, all aspects of life.

Generational theory explains how the era in which a person was born affects the development of their view of the world. Our value systems are largely shaped in the first decade or so of our lives, by our families, our friends, our communities, significant events and, crucially, the dominant mores of the era in which we are born. There is a tendency for people of the same generation to share certain traits and values because they have shared similar cultural experiences.

An assortment of theologians, sociologists, psychologists and business gurus have studied and written about how the growing body of knowledge related to generational theory applies to religious life in general and to Christian churches in particular.[15] The studies among churchless Christians that inspired this book found that, within the responses to some questions related to faith and church, the ways in which people of different generations answered were noticeably different. So, for example, in reply to a question mentioned earlier in this chapter, those born before 1945 were much more likely to indicate that they 'feel part of the worldwide Christian community' (68 per cent) than those born between 1965 and 1981 (30 per cent).

Marital status

In addition to church congregations being contexts where women usually outnumber men, they also tend to be made up predominantly of people who are married. Less than half of over 16s in the UK are married, but three in five of those attending church services are married people. Indeed, those who are in any kind of partnership or are widowed or divorced are more likely to be practising Christians than those who are single. When singles are Christians, they are less likely to be regular church-goers than others. All of these observations were confirmed by an extensive survey of single Christians conducted by YouGov in 2014.[16]

In some congregational cultures, singles feel excluded and misunderstood. As one interviewee explained, 'Single people weren't valued as much. That's what it felt like. That was the perception I got – whether that's actually real, it may not be the case but that's what it felt like.' The YouGov survey found that 43 per cent of Christian singles felt that churches 'didn't know what to do with them'.[17] The survey revealed with stark clarity that singles often feel isolated and lonely in their churches. Reflecting on the nearly

15. Codrington, G. and Grant-Marshall, S., 2011, *Mind the gap!* Bedford, NY: Fig Tree. A business consultant and a journalist have teamed up to produce a helpful and accessible book of generational theory and include a chapter on 'Generations and church'.

16. www.singlechristians.co.uk/info/yougov_report.

17. www.singlechristians.co.uk/info/yougov_report.

10,000 comments received, its lead analyst observed that, while single Christians may feel 'accepted' in church congregations, they often 'do not feel included . . . they feel invisible'.[18]

The degeneration of diversity

If you are as old as I am, you will remember when milk was delivered in glass bottles, sealed with foil caps. I grew up in the countryside and almost every morning, before we collected the milk from the doorstep, a small bird, usually a blue tit, would have pecked through the foil. Those birds couldn't resist a shiny bottle top because in the upper portion of the bottle was a delicious, beak-watering delicacy. To their delight, the milk had settled in the bottle, allowing a thick creamy layer to rise to the surface. These days, when we buy cartons of milk from the supermarket, what we get is 'homogenised milk'. There are no layers. There is no cream. It is all the same, through and through.

You might be thinking that we are rather straying from the point here! However, what the evidence suggests is that there is a phenomenon in churches whereby a kind of 'homogenisation' occurs. Unless it is actively guarded against, a creeping sameness will progressively strangle diversity.

Think back to the way in which you would prefer to get started with a piece of new software or electronic gadgetry. If you are a person who would like to launch in and experiment, you *could* read the manual. However, you would find it boring! If you were forced to read the instructions every time you were faced with a new learning opportunity, you would no doubt become irritated, then frustrated and, eventually, exasperated! If, on the other hand, you are a person who would prefer to read the manual first, but are forced to just dive in and work things out as you go along, you too could probably manage. However, acting against your preferred style, especially if that preference is strongly held,

---

18. Francis, C., 'The singles report', *Woman Alive*, October 2013, pp. 22–4.

would cause you some anxiety. If forced to do it regularly you may adapt, but if your preference for 'manual reading' is strong, apprehension will turn to angst and the urge to escape will intensify.

Likewise, if your natural inclination would be to get some help, being forced to go it alone without support is likely to lead to nervousness or even panic. If your routine required you to act against your inclination week by week, as the next encounter with new technology drew near, instead of looking forward to learning something new, there would probably be a mounting sense of trepidation or dread. Others might even perceive your response as meaning that you don't want to embrace the new opportunities of the latest software or appliance. Disappointed, failing to understand that it is the mode of learning rather than the object of learning that is the difficulty, they may assume a lack of interest and draw back in response. Can you see the 'mutual withdrawal' explained in the previous chapter at work? Can you see here a metaphor for how some people experience church?

Ponder, for example, how a person who is an introvert might experience a church that is led or dominated by extroverts. It is likely that the culture of the congregation will provide a comfortable context for extroverts. Extroverts are more likely to increase their involvement. In contrast, introverts will find the setting to be challenging. They will tend to move to the fringes, decrease involvement and are unlikely to take up leadership responsibilities. If a situation requires you to work against the grain of your natural preferences on a regular basis, it is a stressful place to be.

All the evidence seems to suggest that there is an unconscious, self-perpetuating process which, if unchecked, leads to gradual 'homogenisation'. From rural Anglican churches in Wales to the Scottish Episcopal Church, studies[19] have shown that a few psychological types tend to be over-represented in churches

---

19. Brown, M., 2007, April, *Culture, change and individual differences in the Scottish Episcopal church*. Retrieved from https://openair.rgu.ac.uk/handle/10059/454; Francis, L. J., Robbins, M., Williams, A., and Williams, R. (2007), 'All types are called, but some are more likely to respond: The psychological profile of rural Anglican church-goers in Wales', *Rural Theology*, 5(1), pp. 23–30.

and that there is a corresponding under-representation of other types. Churches that are dominated by a particular age-group will tend to lose members of other age groups and will struggle to involve people of other age groups. Unless an awareness and appreciation of differences within the Christian community are actively cultivated, homogenisation suppresses and diminishes variety.

All one . . . and all different

One of the most wonderful paradoxes of our faith is that, as we follow Christ, 'the Spirit makes us more and more like him'[20] *and* we become the unique individuals we were created to be. In growing into Christ we also grow *together*, proving the validity of Paul's eloquent encouragement that we are 'all one in Christ Jesus'.[21] This is not a question about institutional unity from Paul. It's an unassailable theological fact.

The French philosopher Descartes (he of 'I think and therefore I am' fame) has got much to answer for. That axiom has been etched into Western culture.[22] Rooted in ideas like his and those of others, Western worldviews have become highly individualistic.[23] Philosophers such as Marx, Weber, Freud and Durkheim are being proved right. They all postulated that the growth of rationality and the development of the sciences would result in the rise of individualism and a decline in the influence of religious organisations.

---

20. 2 Corinthians 3:18.

21. Galatians 3:28.

22. In asserting 'cogito ergo sum', Descartes proposed that the mind and body were two separate and distinct entities, the body being a less certain thing than the mind, since it could only be sensed because there was a mind to sense it.

23. Hofstede's Model on National Culture identifies the UK as a highly individualistic society, with a score of 89 on a 0–100 scale of collectivism versus individualism (only exceeded by Australia and the U.S.A.).

It's not just churches. Associations of many kinds are on the wane. Trade union membership in the UK has halved in recent decades and membership of mainstream political parties is at 10 per cent of previous levels. However, while religious institutions may have lost their attraction for most people, Christians continue to be united by the fact that they follow the same Master. One definition of church, as profound as it is simple, is that church is the plural of 'disciple'. The Christian worldview challenges the prevailing Western cultures. It holds more in common with some African cultures, characterised in the Bantu saying, 'I am because we are'.

The worldwide Christian community exhibits some examples of remarkable unity. Tragically, there are also abundant instances of heart-breaking disagreement, discord and division. All who follow Christ are beholden to do all within their power to ensure that the theological truth of 'all one in Christ Jesus' translates into existential reality. For some people that will involve them forging better understanding and links between institutions. This is noble work.

However, the ultimate outcome of Jesus' prayer, 'that they may be one',[24] is not something that can be facilitated by doctrinal statements or church policies. It goes much deeper than organisational structures. It arises as we pursue unity with Christ himself. It is so countercultural and arresting that it makes visible the love of God to the world.[25] Ultimately, the consummation of Christian unity will not be uniformity and a homogenised church. Rather it is portrayed as a countless crowd that exhibits all the differences that comprise the full diversity of humankind.[26] Indeed, our differences are important tools for God's transformation of us, presenting endless opportunities to grow in grace. What a glorious gift to one another we are!

---

24. So important was this petition that Jesus prayed it in triplicate! John 17:21, 22 and 23.

25. Unity has an evangelistic purpose: John 17:23: 'May they experience such perfect unity that the world will know that you sent me and that you love them as much as you love me.'

26. Revelation 7:9.

So what?
Questions and activities
for further reflection

'. . . there is a phenomenon in churches whereby a kind of "homogenisation" occurs. Unless it is actively guarded against, a creeping sameness will progressively strangle diversity.' Have you seen evidence of this? What can be done pre-emptively to counter the process by which one gender, generation or personality increasingly shapes the culture of a congregation?

Consider the theme of this chapter in the light of Jesus' words recorded in Luke 14:12–14:

> Then he turned to the host. 'The next time you put on a dinner, don't just invite your friends and family and rich neighbours, the kind of people who will return the favour. Invite some people who never get invited out, the misfits from the wrong side of the tracks. You'll be—and experience—a blessing. They won't be able to return the favour, but the favour will be returned—oh, how it will be returned!—at the resurrection of God's people'. (MSG)

What practical steps could you take to ensure that your welcome is the proactive 'love of strangers (or outsiders)' espoused by the New Testament?

If you are involved in a church, how might you help the congregation to do all it can to not only be welcoming, but also to be inclusive?

How does remembering 'that there is only one Church, the one, holy, catholic and apostolic Church of the creed, and that local church congregations are a miniscule part of that whole' make it easier to see 'there is room for homogenous units'? What does it mean, in practice in your own situation, to foster 'unity and mutual understanding' *and* encourage opportunities for 'birds of a feather to flock together'.

CHAPTER 6

Our never-changing God – and his ever-changing church?

How can a faith, which is committed to transformation in individual lives and the world, create institutions that are so impervious to change? A survey in the 1990s found that a fifth of church-leavers cited reasons associated with change for their departure. However, more recent studies point to the change-resistant nature of some congregations as being a more significant cause of frustration. This chapter delves behind these findings and searches for explanations for the church's often ambivalent attitude to change.

STRATEGIES FOR RADICAL CHANGE

HOW TO MOVE THE PIANO SLIGHTLY CLOSER TO THE LECTERN

WEEK 1

WEEK 2

WEEK 3

WEEK 4

WEEK 5

WEEK 6

WEEK 7

WEEK 8

Don't copy the behaviour and customs of this world,
but let God transform you into a new person by chang-
ing the way you think. Then you will learn to know God's
will for you, which is good and pleasing and perfect.

Romans 12:2

You've probably heard the joke:

Q: How many [insert the name of a church denomination of your choice]s does it take to change a light bulb?

A: CHANGE???

Funny? Perhaps – but also odd when you think about it. Surely churches should be the very last places to have the reputation of being slow to adapt? And yet they do. They are seen by many as bastions of traditionalism, upholders of the status quo. Indeed, within some traditions resistance to change is viewed as a virtue. How puzzling that an institution rooted in a faith that calls for profound personal transformation, from the inside out, should be perceived as impervious to change. How strange that devotion to a radical revolutionary should give birth to organisations reputed to be stick-in-the-mud and resistant to reform.

All who choose to follow Jesus are called upon to make a dramatic U-turn. The word translated as 'repent' in the New Testament literally means an unequivocal change of heart, a total turnaround in thinking. It is impossible to overstate the depth and scope of the inner overhaul that occurs when someone embraces the Christian faith: 'anyone who belongs to Christ has become a new person. The old life is gone; a new life has begun!'[1] And that's just the beginning! In writing to believers in Rome, the apostle Paul reminds them of the vital necessity of ongoing makeover of the mind. Rather than allowing contemporary culture and the latest fads to shape their character, he calls on them (and us) to allow God to carry out an uncompromising remodelling from within.[2]

---

1. 2 Corinthians 5:17.
2. Romans 12:2.

As those who have committed to a journey of personal renewal, one might suppose that Christians would be especially adept at navigating transition. As organisations that are dedicated to 'proclaiming the gospel *afresh* to every generation',[3] it would be reasonable to think that churches will assume that change is requisite, as they seek to express an unchanging message in an ever-changing context.

A precept of the sixteenth-century Protestant Reformation translates as, 'the church reformed *and always being reformed*'. It reminds us that any form of church that we have experienced is the fruit of centuries of development. It encourages us to remember that continuing modification is imperative. It inverts the popular wisdom, 'if it ain't broke, don't fix it'. In the context of church, 'if it ain't being fixed, it's broke' may be a more appropriate adage. Not that change for the sake of change is ever wise, but because without change, churches quickly become relevant to a context that no longer exists.

All of this requires Christians to be keen observers of our continually changing world. We need to be agile, learning and re-learning what it means to be faithful to the unchanging Christ in a context that is always in flux. Flexibility is a vital element of healthy church culture. Church leaders need to foster a culture where 'always being reformed' is the norm. Crucially, they need to be able to guide and support people as they journey through transition.

'Transition' is not just another word for 'change'. Whereas change is what happens, transition is the response that change evokes in people. Change is tangible, objective; transition is personal, an emotional and psychological reaction. It can be helpfully understood as a three-stage process, with each phase presenting its own particular challenges. First, there is a letting go of what went before. Second, there is that 'gap between the two trapezes' mentioned by a churchless Christian who was quoted in Chapter 4. Like the bulk of an ocean voyage, what's left behind is out of sight

---

3. This is a phrase rooted in the Anglican tradition, but most denominations and traditions would subscribe to the sentiment expressed.

and the destination is yet to come into clear view. Third, there are new beginnings, requiring people to embrace the as-yet unfamiliar. Transitions begin with endings and end with new beginnings. No wonder we can find the journey through change perplexing and emotionally demanding!

If a church decides to dispose of their comfortable chairs and install pews (or vice versa), revise the times of the Sunday morning service or replace the jazz band with an organ, each individual will experience a unique journey of transition. Some people characterise themselves as 'loving change'. Others say they hate it. In reality, we all love some changes and hate others. In general we like *our* changes, those initiated by us or in line with our preferences, and those over which we feel a degree of control. To some extent, our response to change is predicated on understanding the underlying reasons for it. Nobody wants change for its own sake. When it seems like that is the case, or it feels as though it is imposed from 'on high', opposition and conflict are likely consequences.

Ultimately, change is not only part of life; it is a sign of life. Only dead things don't change!

Not change per se, but resistance to change

Researchers have often highlighted the important role of changes within congregations in prompting people to leave. Prior to the *Faith journeys beyond the congregations* study, surveys in the UK typically reported undesired new styles of worship, liturgy and teaching as being key contributors to people leaving congregations. Sometimes these changes coincided with new clergy arriving, but not always. Some pointed to a general dissatisfaction with the direction in which the church was going.[4] Changes to

---

4. Francis, L. J. and Richter, P., 2007, *Gone for good? Church-leaving and returning in the 21st century*, Peterborough: Epworth Press, p. 240.

decision-making structures also appear to be particularly potent in producing negative reactions in some.

The *Church Leaving Applied Research Project* found that, in England and Wales, change within a congregation had posed a major problem to one in every five church-leavers.[5] That study also identified generational differences, with older people apparently more likely to be troubled by changes in their congregation. Of those aged sixty or over, 28 per cent expressed that they did not like the changes that had happened in church, compared with 19 per cent of those in their forties or fifties and 12 per cent of those under the age of forty.[6]

The value of surveys is, of course, dependent in part on the questions asked. Data is gathered only in those areas where the questions probe. Most surveys of church-leavers have asked about the role played by changes to various aspects of church life in their disengaging from church. People were *not* usually asked about issues of resistance to change in churches.

Instead of using a survey, the *Faith Journeys Beyond the Congregations* started with a blank slate and simply asked people to share, in their own words, their experiences of the Christian faith and churches. What emerged as a recurring theme in those interviews was frustration with the change-resistant culture of the congregations. Exasperation with congregations' unwillingness to develop and adapt emerged as a major factor for church-leaving, whereas specific alterations they disliked rarely featured as one of the most significant issues.

Actually, in cases where people did cite a specific change that had occurred, it was often the way that it had been implemented rather than the change itself that had been the cause of disaffection. As one person explained, 'We didn't mind [the change]. It was the way it was done: steamrollering over anyone who got in the way – no consultation, no communication, everything decided from on high.' Another interviewee explained how the

---

5. Francis and Richter, *Gone for good?* p. 244.
6. Francis and Richter, *Gone for good?* p. 245.

poor handling of change undermined their confidence in the congregation's leadership:

[The change] was dealt with very poorly and, unfortunately, [we] found it impossible to come under the authority of the Eldership. [The change] itself was not our reason for leaving – it came down to purely how it was handled.

The experiences of people with church amalgamations, the grouping together of congregations under shared leadership, highlight these as transitions that require particular wisdom in planning and care in implementation. Indeed, research shows that the result of amalgamations is rarely positive. The data shows that the joining of congregations into a common structure accelerates numerical decline – and that this is exacerbated by more congregations being involved. Where congregations have been growing numerically prior to an amalgamation, growth is usually inhibited afterwards.[7] As one interview reported:

The [name of denomination] decided that it was expedient to put together [name of parish A] and [name of parish B] churches as one church . . . I don't think there could be a greater disparity between the congregation of [A] and the congregation in [B]. They were just totally different in many ways, and the [name of denomination] was seeking to join them together to one congregation. It was a recipe for disaster. Everyone seemed to see it except for those making the decisions.

In situations where resources (especially trained clergy) are scarce, mergers appear pragmatic. Indeed, they are often presented as the only reasonable way forward. However, the experience of lay leadership emerging in the context of Fresh Expressions is instructive and shows that alternative strategies are possible.

---

7. Church of England Church Growth Research Programme, 2014, *From anecdote to evidence: Findings of the Church Growth Research Programme 2011–2013*, London: Church of England Archbishops' Council.

More than half of Fresh Expressions in England and Wales are run by lay people. Most have no formal training. Even though the actual number of people involved is still relatively small (about 80,000), the rate of growth is startling. In contrast to the bruising impact of many amalgamations, numerical growth in Fresh Expressions between 2008 and 2013 was almost 275 per cent.[8] People with no prior experience of church are finding faith; people who are already Christians but have been disengaged from congregational life are engaging with expressions of church that are unlike any they have previously experienced.

Not change . . . but the consequences of a lack of change

Let's listen to some of the other voices of Christians who shared their experiences and perspectives during *Faith journeys beyond the congregations* research. Some explained that, in their experience, the way congregations function is often out of step with modern lifestyles and contemporary expectations of good practice:

> One thing I don't like about the church is it has not, I don't think, progressed with time and with society, really. I'm quite dismayed that generally speaking church services . . . have not changed much in 100 years, and that to me is not healthy.

When they expressed dismay at churches' resistance to change, most people were not talking about the theology promoted within congregations. Their source of disappointment was that churches had not evolved in ways that ensured their continued engagement and relevance:

> If there is to be an institutionalised church where people can attend on a regular basis they're going to have to evolve, that's why I don't attend church now. But at the same time I do want my family to know the Christian faith . . . That's why I don't

---

8. Brierley, P., 2015, *UK church statistics 2: 2010–2020*, p. 4, www.brierleyconsultancy.com/images/2014stats.pdf.

go to church now anyway, the lack of evolution in the church makes it impossible for me to look at the church as a serious institution.

Some pointed to the structures and policies of churches that continue unchanged despite changes within their context that have rendered them no longer appropriate. Some mentioned a momentum that seems to be capable of sustaining church structures long after their 'sell by date': '[Name of church] is an amazingly well-designed machine in that it can keep going, keep going, keep going, and I think [that] is part of the problem.'

One couple, reflecting on the years prior to disengaging from church, spoke of a 'time warp' developing as the congregation remained unmoved and unaffected in the midst of a community undergoing enormous developments and cultural upheaval:

We were coming in at the end of an era in a way. I think we were probably one of the last couples of that age to join. And then something happened, in that nothing happened. And it was something of a time warp. I think we had that awareness in the sense that the pattern of worship would've been completely recognisable – and I think largely unchanged – from the 1950s.

Another couple expressed the same phenomenon as church being like a self-contained 'bubble':

I think part of it was the sense of the church exists within its own bubble a lot of the time, and we mix with people . . . we meet people in a shop, we meet people in the course of our work day by day, but it felt often as if these were two separate bubbles that never really involved much integration, and it was hard to imagine what would ever have much impact in the sense of not just 'here we are, this is who we are' but making Jesus relevant to people where they were

Several of the church-leavers I listened to felt that the idea of sitting passively through a sermon was an incongruous format for a task as vital as learning and applying the principles and practices of the faith in the twenty-first century. They longed for more interaction and an acknowledgement that everyone in the congregation had contributions to make. As one person expressed it:

There's more information to consider these days, it's not just about one vicar, and I guess if you look back in history, part of the function of the church was to have a speaker that would educate the population, the congregation, and is that really relevant these days? I don't know, maybe it is to some extent, but we've got more information at our fingertips these days so perhaps it isn't as necessary to come from one man, because you could be blinded by one man's opinion on what it is. I think, generally, as a population we're more educated these days. I think that's fair to say, wouldn't you? So I kind of feel that's one of the reasons why a lot of people don't go.

Just as members of congregations may sometimes feel concern for those who have left, some of the participants in the *Faith journeys beyond the congregations* study expressed their worry for those who have chosen to remain in congregations that are resistant to change:

One of the things we keep encountering is a sense of a watershed that's developing . . . It feels as if God is presenting the church with a choice of either you change and you accept all the risks that go with that change, or you cling onto what's familiar even while it's dying . . . And a number of people that we know have chosen to cling on and have lost even the confidence they had because it feels like the sense of desperation is increasing.

Looking wider . . . and looking for explanations

Just as the findings of a survey are shaped by the questions that are used, so the kind of in-depth interviews used in *Faith journeys beyond the congregations* also have their limitations. These are mainly due to the small sample that is possible. Although that study demonstrated that the issue of resistance to change was an important one for many of those thirty people, whether this was a more widely experienced problem remained a question. For this reason, the *Investigating the invisible church* survey asked a large and scientifically random sample several questions that enquired about peoples' experiences in relation to change and resistance to change in congregations.

Just over a third of the sample of Christians not attending church agreed with the statement, 'The church in this region is in need of radical change'. Baby-boomers (i.e. those born between 1946 and 1964) were more likely to agree (40 per cent) than other generations. In response to a statement, 'I would like to help bring positive change within my local church, but feel powerless to do so', nearly a quarter of those with high scores on the Hoge scale, indicating a particularly strong commitment to their faith, agreed. Just over a quarter of respondents who were born before 1945 said that they would like to help bring positive change within their local church, but feel powerless to do so. Overall 7 per cent of respondents said that they had tried to share thoughts and ideas with their local church but felt ignored. Those who scored highest on the Hoge scale were most likely to have attempted to facilitate change in a local church.

So, the evidence presents a somewhat perplexing picture. Christianity is a faith which, at its core, has a deep commitment to change. Church congregations, the conventional corporate expression of that faith, are called to encourage and facilitate personal change within their members – and to be an agencies for change within wider society. And yet large numbers of previous church-goers have abandoned congregations, after experiencing what seemed to them to be a culture that is impervious to change or inept in its implementation.

Disappointment regarding the lack of change is not usually expressed by respondents in terms of congregations' unwillingness to adapt to their preferences. Rather, it is expressed as a failure to adapt to the surrounding culture in ways that would enable the church to be effective in its purpose. As we search for possible explanations of this paradoxical situation, we need to look at what that purpose is, for it is here, and in the composition and culture of congregations, that we will begin to understand some of the dynamics that are at work.

A Kodak moment?

One of the best documented business blunders of all time relates to Kodak. Despite having invented the first digital camera, they chose not to develop digital photography. They believed that it threatened their existing business. As other companies went ahead and pioneered the technology that would change for ever the way most people take photographs, one of the world's most valuable brands plunged towards bankruptcy. In their blinkered, near-sighted view, decision-makers at Kodak misunderstood the ultimate reason for the company's existence and success. They believed that they were in the photographic film industry, rather than in the business of capturing images and telling stories.

I wonder if those of us involved with church congregations sometimes lose sight of the *purpose* of church, become ambiguous about the nature of our 'core business'. Do we also suffer from a kind of vision-impairing condition and fail to see why congregations, or any church-related institutions, actually exist? I have come to believe that we need to be reminded that church is not the main thing. I suspect that we often make church too important and, consequently, become too precious about 'church stuff'.

From the many accounts of church-leavers, it seems that a fundamental misunderstanding of what church is and isn't, is at the root of much misdirected energy and unnecessary angst. The purpose of church is *not* to perpetuate or grow the church. The raison d'être of the church is *not* the preservation of religious traditions. As followers of Jesus, it's all about him and his Kingdom. Once again, we need to hear that reminder to 'Keep your focus on Jesus'.[9] Jesus himself is the nucleus of the church, the source

9. Hebrews 12:2.

of its life and its reason for being. His Kingdom is our goal, our aim and end.

I'm not being pedantic. This is not theological hair-splitting. It is impossible to exaggerate the importance of the Kingdom in the teaching of Jesus. In the Sermon on the Mount, it is the Kingdom that we are told to 'seek first', to prioritise above all else. As Jesus travelled from village to village he proclaimed the Kingdom by his words and demonstrated it through his actions.[10] In sending out his followers, he instructed them to do likewise.[11] The word 'mission' literally means 'sent' and so we read in the gospels that the followers of Christ are 'co-missioned' (i.e. sent together) to work towards the establishment of God's Kingdom.

Although Jesus never gave a neat definition of the Kingdom, his meaning is clear in the first request of what we often call the Lord's Prayer: 'Thy Kingdom come, Thy will be done in earth, as it is in heaven.'[12]

The Kingdom is not some obscure, esoteric religious concept. In everyday English, a Kingdom denotes the territory over which a king reigns. Similarly, in the New Testament, the Kingdom refers to the realm over which the 'king of kings' exercises his royal authority. All that is submitted to Christ, in line with his will, under his rule and dominion, is part of his Kingdom. As such, we read that the Kingdom is here already (in part), but also still to come (in its fullness).[13] As Christians, after our devotion to God himself, the Kingdom is to be our highest concern.

The misunderstanding of what church is and isn't stems, at least in part, from a distorted concept of how it relates to the Kingdom. They are not synonymous. The Church is intended to be an *agent*

---

10. Matthew 9:35.
11. Matthew 10:7–8.
12. Matthew 6:10 (KJV).
13. According to the New Testament, the Kingdom has both come (e.g. Matthew 12:28 and Luke 17:21) and is yet to come (e.g. Luke 19:11–12). In what is perhaps the pre-eminent theological text on the Kingdom, Professor George Eldon Ladd, explains that the Kingdom of God is both present and future. Ladd, George Eldon, 1959, *The gospel of the kingdom: Scriptural studies in the kingdom of God*, Grand Rapids, MI: Eerdmans.

of the Kingdom, just as we are all invited to be accomplices in God's purposes. However, church is not one and the same as the Kingdom. Some aspects of some church congregations display the characteristics of the Kingdom and others do not. In addition, there is much that is beyond the orbit of church that pleases God, aspects of people's lives and wider society where we can discern the Kingdom of God.

The main thing is that the main thing remains the main thing

The fact that Christianity sometimes becomes church-centred and church-focused, rather than Jesus-centred and Kingdom-focused, is a tragic reality. Churches, like other organisations, have a propensity to drift. There is a tendency for the most important thing to be eclipsed by more peripheral matters. Non-essential issues seem easily to take centre stage.

The catalogue of a Christian resources supplier recently dropped through my letterbox. In large letters, the cover proclaimed 'Christian Essentials'. Below that bold announcement were pictures of candles, church furniture, clerical clothing and specialist communion wine. I have no doubt that all of these things have a valuable place in certain church traditions. However, they are not, by any stretch of the imagination, 'Christian Essentials'.

A German proverb observes that: 'The main thing is that the main thing remains the main thing'. When we fail to abide by that maxim, other things are prone to become substitutes for the 'main thing'. Having being elevated to prominence, these incidentals easily become golden calves which, in time, grow into sacred cows.

Without regular refocusing, repeatedly ensuring that the focus is on the King and his Kingdom and not the church itself, congregations tend to degenerate from being a movement to being a monument, from being dynamic to being static. Eagerness to follow and serve and grow in Christ gives way to routine, monotony and boredom. What was a genuine adventure of faith becomes predictable, humdrum and dreary. All who venture across open oceans or high mountains know the importance of meticulous navigation. Setting off in the right direction is important, but it's not enough. Maintaining the right course through a conscientious routine of checks is also crucial.

Somewhere in the process of drift, the orientation of congregations turns inward. Passion for seeing the Kingdom of God, an earnest desire for 'Thy will be done, on earth as it is in heaven', is replaced by a compliant commitment to 'keep things going'. Dedication to living out the Christian faith and loyal maintenance of the institution become intertwined and muddled. Having moved from 'movement to monument', the next stage is 'mausoleum'. With sufficient resources, religious momentum may sustain a congregation for many years. However, like the sluggish, weak blip of a heart monitor gradually slowing and, eventually flat-lining, energy dissipates and then disappears. The hunger for God and joy in worship and service diminishes. Eventually, the life is gone.

Beware of the rotas

Several interviewees in the *Faith journeys beyond the congregations* study described how, in their experience, a symptom of this deterioration was increasing demands to maintain the institution. One person used the analogy of a vine on a trellis and noted how the emphasis can subtly move from nurturing the organic life for fruitfulness towards maintaining the framework that existed to support it. The structure that was designed to facilitate productivity becomes an end in itself. Increasingly, amounts of time and energy become directed inwards, in 'keeping things going'. The fundamental purposes for the church's existence become fogged or even lost. As one person recounted:

> I was an Elder by then [and] really enjoyed working an Elder's district, it was a great sort of counterbalance to what I'd been doing during the day or during the week, to spend time in a

couple of people's houses and, you know, their experience of life very different from my experience – that was very earthing and I felt people seemed to enjoy the visits, I enjoyed the visits and we were able to . . . I found it was possible to talk about life and faith, and it was natural and it worked, so that was important. But then there was the request for Session meetings, for a Management Committee, there was a hall to be built, there was a lot of time being consumed by all of this and I think that, as we got towards the end of the 90s, what was really striking us were two things – time's short, years are passing by very quickly, this commission that we have to be active in the world as ambassadors for Christ was something that was much more theoretical than practical it seemed.

Around the time that I was interviewing people for that research, a friend came up to me one day and cracked a joke:

Q: Why is the church like a helicopter?

A: Because if you get too close you'll get caught up in the rotas!

Instead of making me chuckle, it made me wince. Having heard too many poignant accounts of how that very phenomenon had led to irritation, frustration, or burn-out, the joke generated a sharp twinge of emotional pain. The words of some who had attempted to address the drift from movement to monument to mausoleum rang in my ears. The accounts of being ignored, isolated or rejected came back to me. I could hear the voices of some of those who have now moved away from being involved in a congregation describing a sense of being 'drawn in' to committees, roles and functions.

Interviewees described experiencing expectations or even pressures to take on responsibilities for which they felt unequipped or in which they had little interest. The assurance of Jesus that 'my yoke is easy to bear, and the burden I give you is light'[14] would suggest that when people find church burdensome and ill-fitting, something is wrong. Perhaps the experience of an onerous and uncomfortable 'yoke' is a symptom of a congregation which is

---

14. Matthew 11:30.

not shaped by the gifts and vision of its people. When there is an expectation to fit into a pre-existing model, a snug fit is unlikely. In terms of the yoke metaphor, chafing and irritation are inevitable. Sometimes the challenge of change requires a stepping back from inherited ways, simplifying things in line with the current reality, being prepared to stop that which has had its day and reshape things around the people whom God brings together today.

Reformed and always reforming?

Over the past decade I have listened to numerous church leaders describe how they find themselves over-extended. They often speak of feeling stretched taut between maintaining contentment and accord in an existing congregation – and responding to the changing context around them in ways that make church accessible and understandable to others. By 'responding to the context', I don't mean to imply a chameleon-like replication of changes in wider society or the mimicking of every fad and fashion. Definitely not. Sometimes the appropriate response is countercultural and involves swimming against the dominant tide. The benchmark when it comes to responding to the context is certainly not a seamless fit. That rallying cry of the reformers, *reformed and always reforming*, was later expanded and clarified by adding the words, '*according to the Word of God*', thus making explicit what was already implicit. Reformation in the context of churches is to grow out of 'double listening', as we give prayerful attention both to the Word of God and to the contemporary world around us. Our '*always reforming*' is to be inspired and guided by our considerations of both Word and world. Only then will we be able to relate one to the other.

In the same way that church leaders often find themselves torn between maintenance and mission, individual church-goers can find themselves torn between fulfilling the demands of their local congregation and being faithful to what they understand is their God-given vocation. In such a case, it is not only a matter of corporate duties becoming unreasonably burdensome. For some they are also a distraction. Such tasks may not be a diversion from the 'main thing' as used above, but they may indeed represent an unhelpful diversion for certain individuals. In response to the *Investigating the invisible church* survey, about one-third of people agreed with the statement, 'Not being involved in a traditional church congregation frees me to pursue what I believe is my Christian calling.'

The teams aren't fair

In their book *Managing polarities in congregations*,[15] Roy Oswald and Barry Johnson share some valuable insights regarding the balance between 'tradition' and 'innovation'. They observe a 'polarity', a tension between opposite tendencies, for stability and change. The desire to honour the past and wanting to be relevant and effective in the present seem to pull in opposite directions. Both poles have their strengths and their downsides in terms of contributing to a healthy, thriving congregation. Like the polarity of 'exercise' and 'rest' for example, over-focusing on one extreme to the total neglect of the other is not a formula for well-being. However, in trying to strike a balance, there is a problem.

Do you remember ever playing a game and realising that the composition of teams was making for a lot of fun for one side and a lot of frustration for the other? And do you remember the evidence mentioned in the previous chapter, demonstrating that church congregations tend to comprise an over-representation of some personalities (psychological preferences) – and a corresponding under-representation of others? Perhaps the strongest data relates to the over-representation of 'sensing' types.

'Sensing' is a term given to the preference for focusing on specific details rather than the wider picture. Those who are less inclined to be sensing are characterised as 'intuitive'. They prefer to focus on the possibilities of a situation, meanings and relationships.

---

15. Oswald, R. M. and Johnson, B., 2014, *Managing polarities in congregations: Eight keys for thriving faith communities*, Plymouth: Rowman & Littlefield.

Put simply, those who prefer sensing are generally conservative and conventional. They favour what is well-known, tried and tested, and well-established.[16] Whereas intuitive types tend to be open to change and innovation, sensing types find the uncertainty and doubt involved to be distressing. Unsurprisingly, empirical research shows that sensing types are inclined to view traditional expressions of Christianity more positively.[17] Christian communities dominated by sensing types are likely to emphasise stability and tradition. They tend to highlight the changeless nature of God.[18]

Overall, sensing types are already more common that intuitive types in European societies. When their over-representation in churches is considered, a picture begins to emerge. The teams aren't fair! A creative tension between Oswald and Johnson's polarities may be an attractive idea, but the reality is often different. For those whose natural preferences put them at the tradition/stability end of their polarity, it is a short step from emphasising the unchanging nature of God to believing that the church too is to be preserved rather than developed. Following God and involvement in church then become tightly entangled. While most people do not occupy an extreme position on the spectrum between sensing and intuition or tradition and innovation, a majority do find themselves in a viewpoint from where it is easier to see the benefits of tradition and the dangers of innovation. Conversely, those who more easily recognise the value of change and the hazards of stability usually find themselves in a minority.

With an awareness that these dynamics exist, steps can be taken to overcome the limitations and risks of our own restricted view.

---

16. Myers, I. B., 2000, *Introduction to type: A guide to understanding your results on the Myers-Briggs Type Indicator* (6th edn, European English version) Oxford: Oxford University Press.

17. Francis, L. J. and Ross, C. F. J., 1997, 'The perceiving function and Christian spirituality: distinguishing between sensing and intuition', *Pastoral Sciences*, 16, pp. 93–103.

18. Francis, L. J., Robbins, M., Williams, A. and Williams, R., 2007, 'All types are called, but some are more likely to respond: The psychological profile of rural Anglican church-goers in Wales', *Rural Theology*, 5(1), pp. 23–30.

Without that appreciation, these differing perspectives easily ignite a battle for the soul of the congregation, each person utterly convinced that the view from where they stand is the whole story.

Because the teams are not fair, with sensing types unconsciously dominating, constancy and convention generally win the day. Innovation is invariably inhibited. Over time, the likelihood is that intuitive types with an inventive streak will be marginalised or will leave. If conflict erupts, there will be collateral damage too. The evidence suggests that sensing types, with their preference for harmony and an aversion to disputes, are more likely to leave because of conflict and how it is handled than because of a frustrated vision for an alternative future.

At a time when many denominations are encouraging creativity and church planting, it is worth noting that some of those most committed to innovation may have left the building. In decades past, an assumption that numerical growth means adding to existing congregations has been dominant in most churches. Increasingly, however, there is an awareness that our contemporary context calls for a strategy of growth by multiplication rather than addition. There is a need to develop a variety of new congregations. Small congregations find growth easier to achieve and, by encouraging assorted expressions of church, diversity can be attained.

In seeking those with an aptitude and vision for initiating Christian community, churches would do well to consider those who are disengaged at the current time. Even within congregations, in view of some of the reflections above, people with an inclination for breaking new ground may well be found among those with a foot in the back door rather than within the leadership team, at the fringes of congregational life rather than in the committed core.

The tendency for agreeable blandness

Of course, pioneering and reform are not the sole preserve of those with a natural bent for entrepreneurism. In my experience, most people involved in church leadership are aware of the need for change on some level. However, in making appointments to leadership positions in mainstream churches, faithfulness in attendance and pastoral gifts tend to be valued over a vision for promoting a culture of learning and development.[19] The implication of this is that, even though a need for change may be recognised, change initiatives run the danger of being choked by compromise.

Allow me to explain what I mean by using the analogy of a family reunion around a shared meal, a not inappropriate metaphor for a church congregation. In such a situation, the last thing anybody wants to do is to offend someone. The over-riding concern is that everyone is happy and that means, among other things, getting the menu right. The challenge is that, like any other assembly of people, this family is made up of individuals, with all their idiosyncrasies. Take Uncle Bertie, for example. He can't eat anything spicy. The saga of that time when chicken vindaloo was served at one of these gatherings is legendary! Then there is Auntie Bessie, whose dislike of red meat is engraved on the memory of all who attended the last family wedding. Young Billy, on the other hand, is never one to pass up a fiery curry or a juicy, pink steak. However, he loathes green vegetables or anything with too many vitamins!

What a challenge! How to please everyone? How to solve this culinary conundrum *and* preserve familial harmony? It's going to require compromise and diplomacy. After much consultation and negotiation, a decision is reached. The grand feast will comprise plain chicken and steamed rice. It's bland, but a safe option. Would anybody at the gathering ever choose this from a menu? Probably not. There is nothing *wrong* with it, but it is boring, insipid and tasteless. Nobody would *prefer* chicken and plain rice, but it is the outcome of their collective disapprovals. It is what everyone dislikes the least! It is a decision that everyone can live with, but which is unlikely to delight anyone.

19. Brown, M., 2007, April, *Culture, change and individual differences in the Scottish Episcopal church*. Retrieved from https://openair.rgu.ac.uk/handle/10059/454.

A culture that is focused *primarily* on consensus and accord eliminates excitement and squashes the quirky, the edgy and the idiosyncratic. By minimising flavour and eliminating spice, what is left is a dreary remnant, a shadow of what could have been. There is nothing wrong with harmony of course. As the Psalmist puts it, 'How good and pleasant it is when God's people live together in unity!'[20] However, the unity created by this sort of process is not the powerful partnership forged by shared vision. It is a disappointing compromise that inspires precious few.

For some people, what they perceive as the blandness of congregational life becomes overpowering. One interviewee, recounting her departure from church as a young person, reported:

I was brought up going to church . . . I found it incredibly boring . . . I found it so boring. I used to faint in church. I never fainted at any other time, but if we were standing up saying some boring creed or something I would feel faint and it was a very physical sensation . . . Anyway, I found it incredibly boring, so I stopped going.

As the remainder of that interview made clear, this ceasing of church attendance was not a rejection of the Christian faith. Rather, it was a realisation that the flavour of congregational worship she had experienced until that point was uninspiring and unhelpful for her: 'I always had a sense of God, I was interested in God, but to me formal religion didn't do it for me, and that remained the case.'

Among the non-church-going Christians who participated in the 2015 *Faith in Scotland* study, the word 'boring' and similar expressions of banality were commonplace. In response to the question, 'What would you say are the main reasons for you not attending church at the current time?', the following were typical of answers given: 'It is a bit boring and should be updated for this day and age', 'It's very boring to be honest', 'The services are really boring and stale'. One in twenty of the sample of over

---

20. Psalm 133:1 (TNIV).

800 people gave similar responses to these. This may not sound like many, but these were people who identified themselves as Christian and who, using their own words, gave similar statements to these as their *main* reason for disengaging with church.

Clearly, in a society that exhibits the 'glorious diversity' explored in the previous chapter, there is a need for a variety of opportunities for shared worship, fellowship and discipleship in order to prevent fragmentation and encourage multi-faceted growth. The voices of Christians who are not engaged with a congregation should prompt churches to foster an ethos of permission-giving, allowing seeds of innovation to be cherished rather than quashed. As former Archbishop Rowan Williams observed, because church emerges from people's encounter with the risen Christ and with each other, there is endless scope for diversity in how that is expressed.[21]

---

21. Williams, R., Feeney, D., Lings, G. and Neal, C., 2004, *Mission-shaped church*, London: Church House Publishing, Foreword.

So what?
Questions and activities
for further reflection

In some traditions, unwillingness to change is seen as a virtue and the role of the church is viewed as changing others by itself remaining unchanging. Why does this chapter argue that reflecting the timeless values of Christ requires churches to be willing to change?

Is there someone you know who is frustrated by the change-resistant nature of a church congregation or another institution? Ask if they would be willing to share their experiences with you. Listen carefully and without judging. Seek to understand their desire for change and the reasons for resistance.

Most church congregations in the Western world are not large. How might a small- or medium-sized community of Christians create space for a range of different approaches to spirituality?

CHAPTER 7

Life really *is* a journey

In describing their experiences of faith and church, people invariably give an account that has all the characteristics of a travel-
ogue. They describe a chronological voyage, peppered with crises
and blessings, encounters and incidents. This chapter explores
how the metaphor of journey, much favoured by spiritual guides,
both ancient and modern, offers a powerful means for making
sense of life's experiences. It investigates how the mistaken notion
that God's interest is reserved for the religious bits of life contributes to changes in church-going.

THE JOURNEY OF FAITH

The Lord *your God has blessed you in all the work of your hands. He has watched over your journey through this vast wilderness. These forty years the* Lord *your God has been with you, and you have not lacked anything.*

Deuteronomy 2:7 (NIV)

The phrase 'Life is a journey' has become such a well-worn cliché that it is in danger of becoming threadbare, losing any real meaning. This is regrettable, because the concept of journey is a potent and evocative metaphor for both life in general and the Christian life in particular. Within the scriptures, journeys provide a rich seam of instruction and wisdom.

From beginning to end, from individual pilgrimages to mass migrations, the Bible is full of people on the move. These travels are often testing-grounds of obedience and a means for shaping character. Faith is usually a prerequisite and is then refined along the way. Abram, for example, was told to up sticks and go. No destination was specified and no road map provided.[1] As when any journey is a following after God, his was not merely a passage from one place to another, but a purposeful expedition in faith. The consequences of his faithfulness (or otherwise) would impact not only him and his family, but 'All the families on earth'.[2] So, no pressure there, Abram!

Bibles often include maps to help us make sense of the migrations and voyages described in the text, many of which were of epic proportions. The Old Testament is criss-crossed with flights from captivity and forced marches into exile, gruelling treks that are depicted as means of discipline, judgement, redemption and transformation. Then, as we read the New Testament, we find God himself undertaking the ultimate journey of humility and sacrificial love, becoming flesh and blood in the incarnation. Jesus himself journeyed into the desert as part of his initiation into a ministry that was characterised by extensive travelling, as he proclaimed

1. Genesis 12.
2. Genesis 12:3.

the good news of the Kingdom with his words and dramatised it by his acts of power and compassion. After his death and resurrection, those who had been Jesus' closest companions on the road were compelled, guided and sustained by God's Spirit to undertake their own journeys, which were often harrowing and treacherous – 'even to the ends of the earth'.[3]

As 'people of the book', we are a journeying people. It should be no surprise, then, that when I asked Christians who are living a life of Christian faith outside the congregational context to tell me their story, they never described a series of random, unrelated events. Their accounts were more like travel journals, as they described a passage through time, interspersed with significant encounters and events, choices and challenges.

For some interviewees, the process of sharing their story with someone who was eager to understand was cathartic, even therapeutic. Occasionally, in the course of unfolding their experiences and sharing their perspectives, there were moments of revelation as a fresh insight came into focus. These moments of epiphany lend credence to the observation of the Danish philosopher, Søren Kierkegaard, who noted that 'Life can only be understood backward, but it must be lived forward'.[4]

I'll not easily forget the moments of sudden comprehension expressed by some of those interviewed for the *Faith journeys beyond the congregations*[5] research. One middle-aged lady, towards the end of her lengthy and intense account, suddenly blurted out, 'The church has got to learn to love again – *that* is it, *that – is – it!*' The emphatic and emotional nature of her outburst spoke of a sudden dawning of understanding. Similarly, an elderly man, looking back to a previously incomprehensible period during which his faith changed from something 'rock solid' to something 'fragile', unexpectedly realised that difficulties in almost every area of life had combined to create a perfect storm of anxiety

---

3. Matthew 28:20.
4. Journals of Søren Kierkegaard IV A 164 (1843).
5. A report, *Investigating the invisible church* is available for free download here: www.resourcingmission.org.uk/resources/mission-research.

('Even now, without any question, that was the worst year of our family life, it really was'). The remarkable thing, which he grasped on reflection, was not that a previously un-critiqued faith, forged in childhood, had taken a severe blow, but rather that its essential core had survived and had later been reinvigorated to become a source of considerable strength and quiet trust.

From the literal epics of Abraham and Moses, through the writings of spiritual guides such as John of the Cross and Teresa of Avila, to modern theories of faith development, there is consensus that the journey metaphor is both pertinent and valuable in making sense of life, especially the Christian life. For those of us who choose to follow Christ, ours is a path of discovery regarding who God is and who we are. Indeed, the two are inextricably intertwined into a single journey of life, faith and everything. It is an integrated whole and leads beyond self-discovery and theology and into growth and change, as we are increasingly animated by the life of God's Spirit and as the character of Christ is formed within us.

If this sounds super-spiritual or highfalutin, don't be fooled. This inner makeover takes place in and through the rough-and-tumble, the everyday, the delightful and the downright horrible. This is a path that we make by walking.[6] It is a road that may seem well-defined and intelligible in retrospect, but where the next step often appears indistinct and perplexing. The power of the journey as a metaphor is that it affirms the role of all kinds of experiences, from the outright joyful to the unquestionably traumatic. It is an effective device for making sense of the multifaceted complexity that is life. Moments of transcendence and times of struggle and tragedy that can seem confounding from the perspective of static doctrine can be understood and appreciated when viewed as part of a unified pilgrimage.

---

6. The phrase 'We make the road by walking' has its roots in a poem in Spanish by Antonio Machado and was brought to the attention of English-speaking readers by the influential Brazilian educator and philosopher, Paulo Freire and, more recently, by Brian McLaren, who took the phrase for the title of his 2015 book on spiritual formation.

Travelogues of the road into churchless faith

In listening to 'churchless Christians', a number of common experiences surfaced which can be explored usefully and meaningfully in relation to the concept of journey. First, the familiar crises of life, such as bereavements, debt, unemployment, sickness and relationship breakdowns, often coincided with times when people reconsidered their beliefs about God and the role of church in their life. Sometimes these became 'tipping points' or 'final straws' for the already disaffected, as explored in Chapter 4. However, others among those surveyed and interviewed recognised that particular crises were catalysts for *beginning* a process of deep re-evaluation and predated any significant sense of disaffection with church.

For example, one middle-aged woman who had been deeply committed to local churches for several decades, had undertaken theological training and had held various leadership responsibilities, described how, after suffering a sudden loss of hearing, she found her faith undermined and experienced a strong impulse to re-examine her beliefs and her involvement in church:

I became suddenly deaf in my right ear. Now that certainly was a life-changing event for me because it meant that I had difficulty with my hearing; clearly, as anyone who is deaf or partially deaf will tell you, that is a very difficult thing – crowded rooms, if there's lots of sounds going on, just talking to people is so, so difficult . . . I was very interested in music. I *am* very interested in music . . . I found that coming to terms with my partial deafness was very, very difficult. I also found that at this time my spiritual life was somehow deadened. I'd lost something . . . I tried to be aware of what was happening and analyse it and it took me several years to work out what was happening . . . I became disenchanted with the church and I felt that I could not really carry on as I was.

Research indicates that experiences of bereavement, the onset of illness and the impact of a personal, local or global tragedy are the most common stimuli for a reassessment of beliefs and practice. While the particular combination of minor mishaps and major catastrophes is unique to each person, these are all commonplace experiences which affect most people to some degree at some point in life. They also tend to be visible to others, which distinguishes them in an important way from certain experiences in what might be called people's private, inner world.

I am not suggesting that there are inner and outer worlds that are distinct. However, the fact that some of life's journey is experienced in an intensely personal way that is invisible from others, whereas 'outer' circumstances and events are often shared with others, does make for differences in the ways it is experienced. The terminology of 'inner' and 'outer' aspects of life is useful shorthand for expressing this. Another reason for adopting these terms is to be faithful to the interviewees whose accounts were a starting point for my own studies. For most of them, too, it was clear that they did not see two journeys, but did recognise two aspects of a single journey.

A second way in which the journey analogy helps in understanding the experiences of church-leavers relates to a growing sense of dissonance emerging between a person's inner journey and their experience of church. More than a third of people surveyed in the *Investigating the invisible church* project reported that 'Changes that happened *within* me led to me stopping attending church.' The development of this perceived gap is cited by many as being at the root of disillusionment and a cause of eventual disengagement.

The way that some of those I interviewed articulated this feeling of a rift opening up suggested a mismatch between what they were experiencing and what was happening, taught or expected in the congregation. Interviewees often reported that, despite previously finding the congregation helpful, church attendance became a chore that contributed little to their spiritual development. About a third of those surveyed in the *Investigating the invisible church* study agreed with the statement, 'I found that attending church did not help my inner spiritual life.' Baby-boomers, those born between 1946 and 1964, are significantly more likely to agree with this than all respondents (42 per cent compared with 32 per cent).

One interviewee explained, for example, that as he grew in faith and had encounters with God in contexts outside the congregation, church began to feel shallow:

There wasn't anything wrong, there wasn't any big fallout or anything, it was just probably what wasn't happening in terms of, perhaps, the 9.30am service was good as it went, but was a bit lightweight . . . Everything was just a little bit lightweight and wishy-washy.

Others, rather than experiencing a frustration with the congregation's depth, described how, for them, a gap emerged when their journey took them through a place of doubt, darkness or difficulty. At a time when they longed for sympathetic companions, confidants who would walk with them and who could help them make sense of what was going on, some people found themselves misunderstood or even marginalised. One person explained her experience like this:

Life got really messy. It wasn't my choice or my doing, but the family seemed to be falling to pieces. I used to have some pretty clear ideas about marriage, divorce and all that, but when things got messy I found it hard to get a right perspective on it all. I got the impression that being a good Christian is expected to mean getting more certain in beliefs and stronger, but I had all these questions and felt all at sea. My belief was there, but I struggled to see how it fitted into this mess that our family was becoming. The message I got at church was that the truth is the truth is the truth, 'you know what God wants', and that I must be losing my faith because I was less regular at church.

In addition to the impact of life's crises and this idea of a rift opening up between a person's inner journey and their experience of church, there is a third way in which the metaphor of journey is prominent within the evidence of recent studies. Interview transcripts and survey findings include many references to a more general disconnect between church and life beyond congregational concerns. The picture that arises is of congregations that are focused on church-related matters and have little constructive to say about the rest of life. One can see how this leads to disaffection among Christians who are passionate about applying their faith in the contexts where they spend most of their time.

One middle-aged man, who had been employed as a church youth worker, voiced his experience of incompatibility between the concerns of his congregation and the issues of people in the wider community. Although he was aware of the interests and issues of young families in the area, he found that the church had no vision to be involved with those things. It was only after he loosened his ties to the church that he found he could connect with the people:

> I'd been conscious of the clash of worlds for quite a while, but it was grating more and more, and though I was an Elder at [name of congregation] I think when I stopped working there is when I started building more on the connections across the church boundary lines again, and enjoying the process.

Eventually, he disengaged from the church entirely after concluding that 'the congregation's only agenda for the community was to get more people to attend church services' and finding that 'the community concerns I became increasingly embroiled in were dismissed as "secular". Unless something was seen as likely to result in people coming to church, it seemed to be viewed as a bit of a waste of time.'

As noted above, one of the riches of the idea of journey is its potential to draw together aspects of life that have sometimes been segregated or pigeon-holed into 'spiritual' and 'secular'. Using a variety of terms, people I have listened to have often referred to a compartmentalisation of life into 'spiritual stuff' and 'the world'. Between a quarter and a third (29 per cent) of those surveyed in the *Investigating the invisible church* study indicated that they felt that 'The church is too negative about the world beyond the church'.

Among those I listened to in the *Faith journeys beyond the congregations*[7] interviews, too, some expressed how concerns or activities about which they were passionate (in some cases seeing these as central to their Christian 'calling'), were seen as outside the realm of interest of the church. These people often expressed a belief that the various aspects of their lives are part of an integral whole and that their Christian faith touches upon it all. However, their experience of church had been that what was right at the heart of their Christian vocation was sometimes perceived as of no relevance, as outside the scope of God's interest.

Reflecting on the findings of the various studies among church-less Christians, I have come to see the concept of journey as invaluable in understanding what, at first, I considered to be three unrelated themes which emerged from the data. First, it can bring comprehension to the often bewildering crises in people's lives. By seeing these as part of a single story, a coherent whole that incorporates both tragedies and joys, the highest highlights and the deepest depths are equally affirmed as part of the journey. Second, the phenomenon of a divergence developing between people's 'inner journey' and their experience of church comes into sharper focus when it is recognised that one's journey cannot be assessed in terms of conformity to congregational norms and that what provides effective nurture differs between seasons of life. Third, if churches do not promote a gospel that touches all of life, or if they promote a differentiation between matters that are considered 'spiritual' and the remainder of life, some of those who are most passionate about the rich totality of life will become disillusioned and disengaged. Such a fragmented and compart-mentalised view of the world presents people with a stark choice of journey. The options are either to pursue a path into increas-ing involvement within the congregation or follow a route that involves an inevitable distancing from the congregation.

---

7. A report, *Faith journeys beyond the congregations* is available for free download here: www.resourcingmission.org.uk/resources/mission-research.

Drawing on ancient wisdom

The notion of life as a journey and faith as a dynamic and evolving element of that is as ancient as the deepest roots of the Judeo-Christian tradition. Led by Moses, the people of Israel were required to travel through the desert and were transformed in the process. That journey from slavery to a promised place of rest, along with its chief obstacles and the Lord's provision, is a recurring motif throughout the rest of scripture.

Across the broad spectrum of Christian traditions, crises, along with their attendant questioning and confusion, have been appreciated as crucibles for transformation and an inevitable aspect of the Christian journey. Indeed, the metaphor of a 'crucible' is apt, as it is a term that has come to mean both a situation of trial and a place in which different elements interact to produce something new.

So, in drawing the attention of readers to the efficacy of a perspective on life and faith as a journey, I am pointing back to ancient wisdom. While some churches have consciously or unconsciously rejected such traditional notions and emphasise instead a growing certainty about a static body of doctrine, there has always been an understanding of faith as something that is refined through adversity. As the intense heat of a forge creates a pliability in iron that was previously cold and rigid, so the doubts and disorientation that often accompany life's crises enable previous convictions to be reassessed and, when necessary, reformed. The extreme temperatures of the furnace not only enable iron to be shaped, but also lead to actual changes in its properties at a microscopic level. Likewise, the refining impact of crises along the road of faith goes deeper than the merely cerebral re-evaluation of beliefs; they become instruments of spiritual formation.

Eminent Old Testament scholar Walter Brueggemann sees this concept of a journey punctuated by trials within the heart cries and petitions of the Psalms, as people who are seeking to follow God move from what he terms 'orientation' through 'disorientation' towards 're-orientation'.[8] In terms of seasons or phases that we travel through in the life of faith, while those offering guidance for the journey adopt a variety of terms from the most ancient to the contemporary, their fundamental concepts are strikingly similar. So, for example, what John of the Cross called 'the dark night of the soul', others have referred to as 'the wilderness experience' or 'desert times'. What Sharon Parks in her work on faith development in young adults calls 'being shipwrecked'[9] is remarkably similar to what Janet Hagberg and Robert Guelich in *The critical journey: Stages in the life of faith* refer to as 'the journey through the wall'.[10]

There are also strong similarities between the earliest traditions and present-day writers regarding what we move *from* and where we travel *to*. One author sees the journey as a movement from 'certainty' to 'intimacy';[11] another speaks of moving from the 'naiveté of faith' through a 'desert of criticism' towards a 'second naiveté'.[12] Based on his work with church-leavers who continue their walk of faith outside the church, Alan Jamieson writes of a passage from 'pre-critical faith' towards a 'post-critical faith'.[13]

While this kind of terminology and the notion of journey can imply a deceptively simple and longitudinal progression, it is crucial to acknowledge that life often takes us through multiple deserts, dark nights or walls. Whatever we call that which we journey towards, this side of eternity it is never the final destination. In that sense, our journey resembles neither a linear path nor a recurring cycle. Rather, as one contemporary author proposes, a more

---

8. Brueggemann, W., 1995, *The psalms and the life of faith*, Minneapolis, MN: Fortress Press.

9. Parks, S., 1986, *The critical years: The young adult's search for a faith to live by*, New York, NY: Harper & Row.

10. Hagberg, J. O. and Guelich, R. A., 1989, *The critical journey: Stages in the life of faith*, Nashville, TN: Word Publishing Group.

11. O'Hare, B., 2004, 'Opening to love: A paradigm for growth in relationship with God' in *Spiritual Direction*, 10(2), pp. 27–36.

12. Ricœur, P., 1967, *The symbolism of evil*, Boston, MA: Beacon Press.

13. Jamieson, A., 2008, *Chrysalis*, Milton Keynes: Paternoster Press.

helpful analogy is a spiral, as we travel through periodic seasons of 'simplicity', 'complexity', 'perplexity' and 'harmony', but they are never the same seasons.[14]

There have been prominent attempts to construct more detailed models of faith development, but these, so far, are unsupported by reliable evidence.[15] While these frameworks have been accepted uncritically by some researchers of churchless faith, a more dependable approach is to affirm simply what has emerged from millennia of lived Christian experience: the simple idea of a movement from a relatively unexamined faith to a deeper and broader perspective via some kind of crisis period or time of doubt or questioning. This is a concept which resonates strongly with the experiences of churchless Christians within my own research, whether that takes the form of understanding the profound impact of a single crisis or the influences of the delights and ordeals of decades. While the validity of the complex models of faith development advanced by psychologists are both uncertain and detached from the concerns and trials of most of us, the modest three-fold representation that has been passed down through generations remains a remarkably effectual and reassuring framework for people who are (like those behind the voices in the section above) seeking to understand what has occurred, what is happening and where it might be leading.

---

14. McLaren, B., 2010, *Naked spirituality*, London: Hodder & Stoughton.

15. James Fowler's work on 'Stages of faith development' has been widely used by those studying the phenomenon of church-leaving. His six-stage model is presented as grounded in research. However, it was never subject to peer review and empirical studies based on Fowler's framework have failed to substantiate it apart from the first two stages, which essentially mirror Jean Piaget's work on childhood development. For further details see: Fowler, J., 1995, *Stages of faith: The psychology of human development and the quest for meaning*, New York: HarperOne; and Wulff, D. H., 1997, *Psychology of religion: Classic and contemporary*. Oxford: Wiley.

Journeying in and out of congregations

If these ideas, identifiable in the narratives of many churchless Christians, are as old as the origins of the faith itself, it raises the question of why crises and their associated processes of enquiry and re-examination should ever contribute to a believer uncoupling from a local congregation. Surely an assembly of believers should provide the ideal setting for wrestling with uncertainties and queries? Surely the care, support and wisdom of others who are travelling the same way would be invaluable? Could not the grappling and tussling of an individual be shared with fellow travellers with mutual benefits?

The answer to these questions is a wholehearted 'yes, but . . .'! Many people *do* find themselves in church congregations where, finding an environment and friendships that nurture them, they thrive and grow. To adopt the imagery used by the prophet Jeremiah, 'They are like trees planted along a riverbank, with roots that reach deep into the water. Such trees are not bothered by the heat or worried by long months of drought. Their leaves stay green, and they never stop producing fruit.'[16] However, the reality is that in the very same congregation there may well be others who find it to be faith-constraining rather than faith-enhancing. For reasons explored in previous chapters, while some may find a congregation welcoming and caring, others may feel excluded or even rejected. Just as increased awareness of differences between individuals and proactive development of a culture of inclusion can lead to a richer experience for all, so cultivating an appreciation of the dynamics of faith within the journey of life will help to facilitate growth in individuals, including an enhanced understanding of others.

The main challenges that the stories of church-leavers bring to congregations are not related directly to programmes and activities; they are matters of awareness and culture. They highlight the importance of building community around certain values rather than any particular brand of theology. People disengage

16. Jeremiah 17:8.

from churches across the full theological spectrum. There is no one denomination or form of church government that has effectively 'closed the back door of the church' (a metaphor that comes across as totalitarian and scary to some people!). Facilitative leadership and excellent communications are important and several 'marks of healthy church' have been identified,[17] but people still leave congregations that conform to every measure of good practice. The simple truth is that, for some, the crises of faith and life take them into seasons of being church-averse. For a small number, this may amount to a sabbatical after which they return. Others will have no intention of engaging with the congregations currently available to them, but still yearn for a different kind of church. The *Faith in Scotland*[18] study found that almost a third (31 per cent) of churchless Christians who had previously been regular church-goers would be likely to engage with a local church 'if there was a different style of church – more like your idea of how church should be'. This figure rose to 42 per cent among those who indicated that their faith was central to their life.

Although some leavers return and others long for a church they would return to, the majority of churchless Christians remain detached, but often find other forms of Christian community, whether face-to-face or virtual, structured or informal. As explained in Chapter 2, the data establishes that the majority of 'churchless Christians', whether they were previously church-goers or not, are contentedly non-congregational. Many indicate that they prefer to live out their faith without reference to religious institutions. For example, within the *Investigating the invisible*

---

17. For example: the 'seven marks of a healthy church' expounded in Warren, R., 2012, *The healthy church handbook*, London: Church House Publishing; the 'eight essential qualities of healthy churches' espoused in Schwarz, C., 1996, *Natural church development*, Saint Charles, IL: Churchsmart Resources; the 'six characteristics of a healthy church' outlined in The Church of Scotland's 2001 *A church without walls* report available at www.churchofscotland.org.uk/__data/assets/pdf_file/0006/11787/CWW_REPORT_for_website_2Nov2012.pdf.

18. A report, *Faith in Scotland*, is available for free download here: www.resourcingmission.org.uk/resources/mission-research.

church study, just over two of every five respondents (41 per cent) agreed with the statement, 'I want to follow my own spiritual quest without religious institutions'. Paradoxical as it may seem, it seems that characteristics of a healthy church culture include an awareness that sometimes people *need* to leave, grace to allow people to part with a blessing and a determination to maintain open communication and loving relationships throughout.

Mind the gap

Having explored how the insights of our ancestors in faith continue to enable a greater appreciation of the sometimes baffling ebbs and flows of life, we now turn to another ancient concept. Sadly though, in this case, rather than being a source of wisdom, it is a fallacy. It is an error that has endured through the centuries and which lies at the root of the disconnect between congregational concerns and the common affairs of life.

As I write this chapter I can hear unusual sounds of heavy machinery. Within a few hundred metres of my home is the A9, the arterial road of the Scottish Highlands, and the section closest to my office is being 'dualled'. After years of debate, it is being 'upgraded' and will, in future, be a dual carriageway. Throughout history there have been influential proponents of the conviction that our understanding of ourselves and the world would be 'upgraded' if it was 'dualled'. Among history's most prominent and persuasive thinkers there have often been advocates for the idea that we live in a world where subject and object are independent of each other, and mind and body are distinct. This may seem rather esoteric and irrelevant to the concerns of this book. However, the outworking of these concepts has had a substantial influence on how people perceive the world.

The way life appears to us depends on the assumptions that we hold. We all have what behavioural scientists have termed a 'worldview', a set of presumptions, which operate as a lens through which we see everything. The presuppositions that form our worldview seem so logical and obvious to us that we are usually unaware of them. Rather like those of us who have become used to wearing glasses or contact lenses, our vision is modified, but usually unconsciously.

When we view life through a lens that is tainted by 'dualism'[19] the consequence is 'split vision'. Instead of seeing a unified whole, we see the world as a series of dichotomies. Crucially for Christians, over the centuries, dualism has led to a distorted and fragmented vision of life. Aspects of life have been branded as 'spiritual' or 'worldly', 'sacred' or 'secular', 'holy' or 'profane'. In the previous chapter we saw how the change-resistant culture of some congregations leads to them becoming disconnected from their communities and perceived as lacking in relevance. The pervasive and adulterating split vision of dualism has the same pernicious effect.

One interviewee explained it this way:

By the late 80s [we had] a much more conscious understanding of the mismatch between church and most of where I spent my life and [name of spouse] was an [occupation] and so we were both busy Monday to Friday . . . And so the whole world of work was like a complete blind spot. There was nothing direct coming through church to help one understand the challenges and the complexities . . . this sense of disconnect continued to develop and it became clear that we were in a kind of odd position where a lot of our life, the two of us together, fitted quite well, was quite coherent, and the one piece that should be at the centre of the jigsaw – our church life – was actually in some ways the one piece of the jigsaw that fitted worst.

This extract is from the account of someone who has a deep-seated belief that his business is central to his Christian vocation.

---

19. In using the term 'dualism' (small 'd') my intention is to communicate its ordinary meaning of 'a division or contrast between two things that are represented as being opposed or entirely different' – as opposed to the more specific ways in which 'Dualism' (capital 'D') has been used by various schools of philosophy. In the sense in which I use it here, it refers to a worldview that sees things in terms of dichotomy.

He longs to develop working practices and business tactics that are shaped by Christian principles and values. However, after many years of finding that the substantial involvement he and his wife had in a local church detracted from their vocation rather than enriched it, with heavy hearts, they withdrew from the congregation.

Insights gleaned from interviews like the above are confirmed by data from surveys of larger, random samples. Of the church-less Christians surveyed as part of the *Investigating the invisible church* study, 37 per cent agreed that 'sermons in church have little or no relevance to my everyday life'. As well as asking respondents about how they perceived the church to be relevant to themselves, the survey also explored their thoughts about the relevance of church to other people. So, for example, in response to the statement, 'Church feels like "another planet" to most people', nearly half (48 per cent) agreed and less than a quarter disagreed.

Like Japanese knotweed, the sacred–secular divide that arises from a dualistic worldview is invasive. It spreads, dominates and is dreadfully difficult to eradicate. Despite determined attempts by the most prominent reformers (Luther and Calvin both explicitly challenged a dualistic worldview), it continues to distort and corrupt. Symptoms of split vision in the church are seen whenever some tasks or jobs are seen as 'sacred' and others ruled as 'secular'. When congregational prayers focus on missionaries and Sunday school teachers, but exclude those whom God has led into service within the police, the local primary school, bakery, pub, supermarket (the list is endless) we, in effect, deny God's interest in, and sovereignty over, the whole of life.

In behaving as though times and places are divided into 'the spiritual' and 'the rest', we contradict Christ's own confession about himself when he declared 'I have been given all authority in heaven and on earth'.[20] As the Dutch theologian, Abraham Kuyper, stated with unpretentious simplicity and absolute clarity,

---

20. Matthew 28:18.

there is 'not a square inch' of the universe over which Jesus Christ does not exclaim "Mine!"'. As if to underscore the implications of his statement, Kuyper was both a minister of religion and, for a few years, Prime Minister of the Netherlands!

Affirming a fundamental unity over a deceptive dualism is not, of course, the same as suggesting that all things are equal in God's sight. Not everything in this pulsing cosmos of spirit and matter gives God an equal joy. However, this is entirely different from a distinction between, for example, places (e.g. church = holy, office = secular), times (e.g. Sunday morning = spiritual, Monday morning = ordinary) or jobs (e.g. working for a Christian charity = sacred, working for a bank = worldly). These kinds of distinctions lead to a vision of life which is both shrunken by short-sightedness and degraded by narrow-mindedness. In contrast to this sort of fragmented view, God's vision is that, in Christ, 'all the broken and dislocated pieces of the universe – people and things, animals and atoms – get properly fixed and fit together in vibrant harmonies, all because of his death, his blood that poured down from the cross'.[21]

To resist dualism and uphold God's concern for, and involvement in, the entirety of existence in no way degrades or derides spheres of life that the dualistic view considers sacred. Rather, by affirming that all are equally valuable to God and therefore the legitimate focus of our endeavour, it asserts that *every* domain and every task is potentially magnificent, wonderful and extraordinary. Paul, writing to Christians afflicted by heresy, implored them to 'Let every detail in your lives – words, actions, whatever – be done in the name of the Master, Jesus, thanking God the Father every step of the way.'[22,23]

---

21. Colossians 1:20 (MSG).

22. Colossians 3:17 (MSG).

23. Some scholars argue that the deceptive teaching in Colossae shared some similarity with the dualism discussed here – see McRay, J. in Elwell, W. A. (ed.), 1996, *Evangelical commentary on the Bible*, Grand Rapids, MI: Baker, p. 1050.

Visible signs of change

At a time like the present, an era of cultural flux, Christians of the Western world need to listen to, and learn from, the insights of people like the church-leaver quoted above. In articulating their frustration with the way some congregations promote a segregated view which fails to recognise the interconnectedness and fundamental unity of life's journey, such people offer a prophetic and vision-enhancing word to all who have ears to hear. It is striking that one of the common characteristics of groups formed around 'churchless Christians' is a vision for engagement with the totality of life.

Many of these groups recoil from the term 'church' and talk more, for example, of 'getting together with others', 'meeting up to support one another', or 'gathering to pray and share'. However, as I have listened to the people involved describe what it is these 'gatherings' and 'groups' aspire to be and to do, their accounts are strongly suggestive of that mutuality urged in the numerous 'one another' exhortations of the New Testament which we touched upon in Chapter 3. I certainly don't mean to imply that every Christian who is not engaged with a church is immune to, or has been liberated from, a dualistic worldview. It is striking though that many of these people cite an experience of disconnection between church and life as a main or contributing factor in their deciding to remain outside of traditional congregational life.

In relation to the concerns of this chapter, it is encouraging to see resurgence in traditions of spirituality that are characterised by a strong emphasis on journey and where the sacred–secular divide is conspicuously absent. Celtic Christianity, for example, has experienced a notable renaissance in recent years. With its emphasis on the Christian faith being woven into the very fabric of life, it offers a refreshing antidote to a fragile dualism. Perhaps, being relatively unscathed by the assumptions of Christendom (see Chapter 2), it is better equipped for a contemporary world which has largely dismissed those suppositions than expressions of church that have been shaped within it.

The term 'new monasticism' has been coined to describe an upsurge in people embracing the emphasis on intentional community, patterns of prayer, and a commitment to hospitality associated with monastic traditions. In an important divergence from many of the ancient orders from which this recent movement draws inspiration, it emphasises the scattered life of the Christian community. While community members may gather frequently, their dispersal throughout ordinary living and working environments for the majority of time is seen as positive and celebrated as presenting opportunities for being 'salt and light' in these places.

Another unexpected and promising movement, congruent with the metaphor and reality of journeying, is the remarkable revival in recent years of pilgrimage. The signs are clear to see: new pilgrimage routes are opening up, there is a plethora of fresh literature, footfall at pilgrimage sites is at an all-time high. Rather like the new monasticism, contemporary pilgrimage is rooted in rich pre-reformation traditions, but is also distinct from them. In her book, *Soulfaring: Celtic pilgrimage then and now*,[24] Cintra Pemberton suggests that, whereas pilgrimage in the Middle Ages was 'almost without exception church-related', the tide of present-day enthusiasm originates from a widespread disillusionment with the institutional church. Pemberton believes that much modern pilgrimage is undertaken as a way of assuaging a spiritual thirst that, for many people, cannot be quenched by the church.

In pointing to the re-emergence of pilgrimage as a positive sign, you may feel that I am contradicting myself. Surely by encouraging journeys to so-called sacred sites, pilgrimage is both rooted in, and perpetuating, the same deceptive dualism I have just cautioned against. However, as Pemberton's analysis shows, the motivation for pilgrimage and its focus have undergone fundamental re-orientation throughout history. For pilgrims of the Celtic age the purpose was primarily evangelistic and mission-orientated. In the Middle Ages, pilgrimage centred on religious relics, such

---

24. Pemberton, C., 1999, *Soulfaring: Celtic pilgrimage then and now*, New York: Morehouse, pp. 45–6.

as the bodily remains of saints and artefacts associated with them. Pemberton argues that modern pilgrimage is centred on healing and wholeness, inspired by a craving for reconciliation between humans and with their environment, and by a longing for restoration of lives that have become fragmented and compartmentalised.

Sites renowned as 'thin places', locations traditionally understood as where the veil between the spiritual world and our own physical world is unusually permeable, continue to influence the choices of route and destination of devotional wayfarers. However, the typical hope of travellers today is less for blessing from an endpoint deemed to be sacred and more for a journey which results in a sharpened perception of God's presence and activity in the commonplace and the ordinary.

So what?
Questions and activities
for further reflection

Starting from the present and working back, draw a map of your journey through life thus far. Highlight places where key choices occurred. Include any churches you have encountered.

Looking at the map of your journey, can you recognise 'seasons' of 'simplicity', 'complexity', 'perplexity' and 'harmony'? What have been the influences of churches?

Who have been key people who have influenced you along the way? Look particularly at the main 'junctions' or 'crossroads' when your life could have taken another direction. Are there people you want to thank? Are there people you need to forgive?

Pray for a greater awareness of the sacred–secular divide in your own thinking.

If you are part of a church, listen for whether the activities or language of congregational life suggest a sacred–secular divide or encourage a strong integration between church and the rest of life.

Are there developments that would make shared times as a congregation better integrated with the rest of life? What could be done to develop greater awareness of the congregation as the dispersed community of believers that they are for most of the time?

CHAPTER 8

Learning to love

The night before his death, aware of all that was to come, in the
tense atmosphere of that upper room, Jesus turned to his followers
and said '*this* is how everyone will know that you are my disciples'.
The 'this' was not a new doctrine; he was not referring to any of the
symbols we associate with Christianity today. The 'this' was, quite
simply, love. Simple it may be, but never easy. This chapter reflects
on evidence which suggests a need to rediscover the priority of love.

HE HAD BEEN THERE FOR FOUR YEARS,
BUT THE OTHER CHURCHGOERS ASSUMED
HE ARRIVED EARLY AND LEFT LATE

I am writing to remind you, dear friends, that we should love one another. This is not a new commandment, but one we have had from the beginning. Love means doing what God has commanded us, and he has commanded us to love one another, just as you heard from the beginning.

2 John: 5–6

Love one another

These few words from John's second epistle brought with them a rebuke so sharp that it left me feeling winded, reeling from the implications of what I had just realised. As is often the case, what I suddenly grasped was neither original nor indeed new to me. However, it dawned on me afresh in a way that confronted my perceptions of church and my personal priorities.

I had been asked to contribute some reflections on John's letters for a series of daily Bible notes and had been reading carefully through these brief but remarkable epistles in a variety of translations and paraphrases. At the time my core work entailed working with a number of local congregations, helping them to review what they were doing and to discern the way ahead for the coming years. Typically that involved discussions about leadership, structures, training, engagement with the wider community, activities for different age groups, worship styles, the practicalities of timetabling and buildings: the brass tacks of church as I understood them. I was well versed in theories of church growth and familiar with various ideas of what constitutes a healthy congregation. I had a tool box overflowing with resources and activities to enable congregations to understand and implement principles, which, I was confident, would lead to improvement and growth. And then I read these words of John.

John was an old man by the time he wrote this letter. He was the last surviving member of the original group of apostles. The Church was vulnerable like at no other time in its history. The last eye-witnesses to the life, death and resurrection of Jesus would soon pass away. The Bible as we know it now had yet to be formalised. Peripatetic teachers and prophets were an increasing and necessary part of the church scene. Most were sincere and devoted. However, there were others who were frauds, scammers posing as prophets, in it for an easy living.[1] So, as John picked up his quill, he was concerned. What would he write to this fledgling congregation?[2]

It really was going to be a quick note, a single side of a standard sheet of papyrus. He would need to be selective, to focus on what he believed to be the most crucial matter, the issue of paramount importance. The verses at the head of this chapter reflect the heart of what he decided to write. John's letter restates and reinforces something that he had heard many years earlier from the lips of Jesus: 'I am writing to remind you, dear friends, that we should *love one another.*' After a lifetime of reflecting on the teaching of Jesus, John reckoned love to be the hallmark of healthy Christian relationships, the touchstone of authentic Christian fellowship.

This is why I felt admonished on re-reading these verses. I had enabled numerous churches to examine the fundamentals of their plans and programmes. I had assisted them in drawing up mission statements and advised them in carrying out community audits. However, I had never once directed their attention to the heart of the matter, as John saw it. I had failed to remind them of the uncomplicated and yet also the most demanding of Christ's commandments for all who follow him: 'love one another'. As I heard John's words anew, I recognised that, whatever challenges a church faces, reinforcing this foundation is always the right

---

1. The Didache, the earliest 'instruction manual' for Christians, coined a word for such people: 'Christmonger' – someone who *traded* in Christ. For them, 'prophet' equated to 'profit'.

2. Considering how little ink was required to write this letter, it is incredible how much has been spent debating to whom it was addressed. Some suggest that it was written to a woman and her family, but most scholars see this as a letter to a church. So Eugene Peterson begins his translation, 'My dear congregation' (MSG). This understanding makes 'the children' members of that local Christian community.

starting point. It has been said that 'One of the pleasures in reading old letters is the knowledge that they need no answer',[3] but this ancient epistle demands a response. It compels us to search our hearts and re-evaluate our attitudes, relationships and actions.

We shouldn't be surprised to discover John's conviction regarding the unqualified primacy and priority of love. After all, in his first letter he makes the astounding affirmation that 'God is love' (1 John 4:8). In that astonishing assertion he doesn't merely state 'God loves' or that 'God is loving', but rather he proclaims that 'God *is* love', stressing that love is his very essence. The consequence is that everything God does flows from his fundamental nature, which is love. So many theological dilemmas are resolved when we start from this foundational truth. Like a mathematical equation that becomes solvable only when we are told the value of x, many of our difficulties dissolve when we take as our starting point the fact that 'God is love'.

Because God is love, it is unsurprising that 'God in flesh', Jesus Christ, and his first followers should insist that love must be the defining characteristic of his people.[4] From the earliest days of the Church, the clear manifestation of love in the relationships between Christians and the ways in which they show sacrificial love to others have testified to the transforming presence of God. So, for example, in the early third century, Tertullian noted the amazement of the pagans of his day as they observed the Christian community: '"See," they say, "how they love one another . . . and how they are ready to die for each other"'.[5]

---

3. Often attributed to the English poet, Lord Byron (1788–1824), but according to the *Oxford Dictionary of Humorous Quotations* (Brandreth, G., 2013, Oxford: Oxford University Press), this is 'probably apocryphal' (p. 179).

4. John 13:34; 1 John 3:23.

5. The full quotation reads: '"Look," they say, "how they love one another" (for they themselves hate one another); "and how they are ready to die for each other" (for they themselves are readier to kill each other)'. This is usually quoted as 'See how [these Christians] love one another'. It is found in *Apologeticum* Ch. 39, 7. CSEL 69, trans. Glover, T. R., 1931, Loeb edition, Cambridge, MA: Loeb Classical Library.

What's love got to do with it?

While most of us would recognise the prominence of love in the teaching of the New Testament, we might be tempted to think that it is too abstract a concept to be of benefit in investigating the invisible church, the central concern of this book. Surely, how people experience love is entirely subjective? After all, who is able to ascertain whether or not behaviour and actions are motivated and energised by love? How could it ever be possible to discern the presence or absence of love? In considering the health of a church, few would doubt the importance of love, but some would certainly question the practicality or value of examining something that is so non-concrete. While love is certainly neither immaterial nor imperceptible, is it really assessable?

However, we *do* assess love. Indeed, while evaluating love may be performed chiefly in ways that are intuitive and unintentional, it is arguably one of the most imperative and frequent evaluations that we make. To be human is to have both the capacity to give and receive love and the *need* to do so. Whether we like it or not, we are attuned to factors that we consider to be indicators of love. Consider Paul's description of love in his letter to the church in Corinth:

> Love is patient and kind. Love is not jealous or boastful or proud or rude. It does not demand its own way. It is not irritable, and it keeps no record of being wronged. It does not rejoice about injustice but rejoices whenever the truth wins out. Love never gives up, never loses faith, is always hopeful, and endures through every circumstance.[6]

While we may not often give conscious consideration to whether or not we experience love, we *do* know when we experience patience and kindness. Likewise we recognise when we are on the receiving end of jealousy, boasting, pride and rudeness.

---

6. 1 Corinthians 13:4–7.

Where there have been more deliberate and objective attempts to evaluate love in the context of church congregations, findings have been suitably modest in their claims, but profoundly insightful nonetheless. For example, the Institute for Natural Church Development (NCD),[7] in the most extensive study of its kind, has sought to identify principles of church growth which apply across cultures and regardless of theological persuasion. The institute has analysed more than four million survey responses from more than 70,000 churches worldwide and, as a result, has identified 'quality characteristics' that have a strong association with congregational health and numerical growth. This empirical evidence demonstrates that churches that are growing numerically score more highly on twelve factors associated with 'loving relationships'[8] than stagnant or declining churches.

Conversely, where survey responses indicate a lack of loving relationships, church development is 'severely hampered'.[9] Among larger churches, of all the eight 'quality characteristics' identified by NCD, 'loving relationships' is most frequently the lowest scoring. This final point coincides with the findings of multiple studies around the world which consistently show that the size of congregations is a crucial factor in congregational health and numerical growth. Put simply, it is more likely that a smaller church will grow than a larger one. For example, within the Church of England, between 2006 and 2011, small churches (0–14 and 15–29) showed the most positive growth trends whereas congregations of 50–300 tended to decline.

The fact that churches which are larger still (300+) are more likely to grow may seem to contradict the idea that smaller congregations grow more easily. However, these larger churches invariably develop an effective network of cells or small groups, giving

7. www.ncd-international.org.

8. For example, respondents were asked about their experiences within the congregation of joy and trust, interdependent relationships, affirmation and encouragement, intentional conflict resolution.

9. Schwarz, C., 1996, *Natural church development: A guide to eight essential qualities of healthy churches*, St Charles, IL: Churchsmart Resources, pp. 36–7.

people the regular experience of a small congregation. Indeed, NCD's studies show that the larger a church becomes, the more decisive the role of small groups. Although the institute emphasises the interaction of *all* of the 'quality characteristics', the multiplication of small groups is the most important single factor. The strategic benefits of small groups are manifold, but their contribution to congregational health and growth is in no small measure related to the context they provide for fostering loving relationships.

Of course there is no 'right' size of church. However, the fact that, in the Western world at least, churches tend to be of medium size,[10] means that they are caught in the gap in terms of the advantages and drawbacks of smaller and larger congregations. They often lack the intimacy of the small and are also unable to benefit from the resources and diversity of the large.

The power of love

In listening to Christians who are not engaged with a church congregation, I did not, at first, recognise the centrality and importance of their experiences of giving and receiving love. However, the impassioned and revelationary outburst quoted, in part, in the previous chapter, caused me to review again the recordings and transcripts of other interviews:

I'm really – stopping myself because I can just hear myself what I've said, that the love – is because there isn't love. It's actually

---

10. In the USA, the National Congregations Study estimated that smaller churches draw only 11 per cent of those who attend worship. Meanwhile, half of all church-goers attend the largest 10 per cent of congregations, which includes churches with 350 or more regular participants. Therefore, 90 per cent of churches have fewer than 350 attendees. In the UK there are a number of churches with multi-thousand congregations (mainly black Pentecostal churches). However, the average size for a Sunday congregation is around eighty-five and the most common size of church congregation is in the thirties.

because there isn't, that people are sitting outside the church. Do you know, I actually realised that is it. I'm feeling it in my heart, because I'm saying it out loud. I hadn't actually thought it as conclusively as that. There is not the love. In the church if the love of Christ is really not coming through from top to bottom . . . The church has got to learn to love again – *that* is it, *that – is – it*!

How had I missed it first time around? Interviewees spoke of how their experiences of love had led them to Christian faith and, in some cases, church involvement, in the first place. Some spoke of how the lack of love they experienced contributed to their disengagement from a congregation. Those who had never been regular church-goers spoke of how their decision not to join a local congregation was influenced by a perceived deficit of love. As will be explored more in the following chapter, for some interviewees, it was a love for others that actually led them to walk away from any congregational expression of church.

The following are representative of statements about the vital role of love in the beginning of their Christian experience and, in some cases, their church-going life. They come from men and women of different generations. They had varying experiences of church, but all are currently disengaged from any congregational involvement. One middle-aged woman described the realisation of God's love for her while participating in a lively service of worship:

I would listen to praise music and actually hear the words, and there were things like arrows at times just going into my heart, you know, the messages that he was giving me, the love that he was pouring out in some of the songs.

A middle-aged man described how his experience of love within the context of a Christian family awoke a longing for the faith that he saw at work in them:

I visited just for a week, and I was so impressed by the love between the Christians – they would eat together, and they would care for each other, they had joy and they had peace. I was so impressed by their lifestyle that I started to ask questions during that week. And I had many questions. Some of my questions were answered, others weren't answered, but I came to the point during that week at which I asked God to forgive me and I asked him to give me a new life.

One young woman spoke of encountering the love of God when she went along to a church at a time of particular crisis in her life:

I was going through this trauma . . . I started going back to this 'happy clappy' church, if that's what you want to call it, because it was very happy and it was very clappy! But that was a completely different experience – I could see faith being more of a lifestyle and something more real than what my previous experiences had been. I'd never heard of this thing called the Holy Spirit, but they were all actively moving in the Holy Spirit and there was things like messages that sounded like gobbledygook but I believe was tongues and I was completely . . . it was a new experience and it just blew my mind really. But I could feel, actually, this is what I wanted, because there was so much love and all the rest of it – things that I'd been looking for but hadn't known that's what – I felt as if I was home in that place. I went to prayer meetings and everything when I got involved in that.

For one young couple, responding to an invitation to attend church at a time of personal need resulted in an encounter with a loving community, in which they encountered the love of Christ:

So we woke up the next morning and we were awake with enough time to go, so we went along and as soon as we got in the room people started talking to us, without knowing the circumstances that were going on and just instantly I just felt loved and cared for and it was just . . . yeah, people just kept talking to us – we could hardly get out the door.

A tragic anomaly

Sadly, while love within the context of Christian community was often prominent in interviewees' explanations of how and why they embraced the Christian faith and, in many cases, committed themselves to involvement in a local congregation, it was often a perceived lack of love that contributed to or sealed a decision to disengage. Some people described being hurt by unloving behaviour or a dearth of love over a period of time. For example, one young woman found that, during a lengthy time of particular difficulty and need, the congregation were uncaring and she felt wounded by that:

> I'm out of contact with church through illness but I was very badly handled as I was getting ill . . . I carried on, determined, long after it became detrimental to my health to carry on. I believe in the importance of Christians gathering. I miss church – the good side – very much. But it was a relief in the end to leave . . . I love Jesus more than ever and I couldn't have survived a minute of what I've been through without him. My faith is growing. What is it with church? It can be brilliant, even traditional denominational churches where the structures are used wisely and where there is fellowship of some sort among the members. And yet . . . I have contact with a few Christians on Facebook which I have found helpful on the whole, though some got so hurt they can be very negative about 'institutional' Christianity and I find that discouraging 'cos church can be brilliant. I miss it. So I find these days I spend more time sticking up for it despite my experiences!

More often than referring to unloving behaviour towards themselves, interviewees cited the lack of love shown to others within congregations as prompting their own disillusionment. For example, one elderly man recounted a catalogue of incidents that he had witnessed at close quarters – including, for example, the 'appalling handling of a situation' when a church leader 'experienced a personal crisis in her ministry' and a 'congregation . . . split in two' when a minister resigned over denominational policy – and concluded, 'Where is the compassion and the love of Christ in any of these examples?'

One of the people quoted above, whose experience of love had drawn them into faith and church, later found herself in a (different) congregation where loving relationships appeared all but absent:

> To think about church to me is to be in a loving family and I'm just not sure that an expression of church is a place where there's kind of no accountability to anybody, there's no-one asking how your week's been. Sorry, in church there are people asking you 'How's your week been? What are your struggles?' – connecting and engaging with your life and I would admit I didn't go in there asking people how they were doing as well, but to go in as a new person I would just have anticipated somebody speaking to me . . . So I guess I struggled with the feeling that I could be completely hidden in a room full of people saying that they loved each other.

One young man described how he felt 'embarrassed – yeah, even ashamed' to be part of a church because of the way that congregation was experienced by his friends, neighbours and work colleagues as 'judgemental, negative – yeah, just having nothing positive to say to the people round about'. At the heart of his growing disillusionment with the church was the sense that relationships in the congregation were characterised by:

> A kind of false chumminess, but no real depth. The only thing that seemed to join people together was their believing the same stuff. I was treated as an insider, but when I heard what some people said and what they did, I didn't want to be an insider.

Having left the congregation, there were two thoughts that were helpful in understanding why he had become disaffected:

Love is between people. Nobody loves institutions and nobody loves others because they are a member of something. In my mind the church should be like a lighthouse in the community – spreading truth, love, doing good. What I see here is a church that, instead of spreading light, casts a shadow. I'm sad when I say that.

The testimony of interviewees and respondents to surveys confirm that Christian communities have the potential to demonstrate love in ways that reflect the character of Christ himself and lead to personal transformation. However, this data also indicates that some churches develop cultures where both newcomers and existing members sense a disappointing discrepancy between the loving behaviour commanded and commended in the New Testament – and reality. Indeed, when such congregations are viewed through the lens of Christianity's foundational scriptures it can only be concluded that they are fundamentally flawed. Without love the most highly developed strategies and the most finely honed programmes are futile. In fact they are worse than useless. As Paul tells us in his letter to the church in Corinth, when activity is not inspired and animated by love, it is like an annoying noise. As Eugene Peterson expresses it in his translation of 1 Corinthians 13:

> If I speak with human eloquence and angelic ecstasy but don't love, I'm nothing but the creaking of a rusty gate. If I speak God's Word with power, revealing all his mysteries and making everything plain as day, and if I have faith that says to a mountain, 'Jump', and it jumps, but I don't love, I'm nothing. If I give everything I own to the poor and even go to the stake to be burned as a martyr, but I don't love, I've gotten nowhere. So, no matter what I say, what I believe, and what I do, I'm bankrupt without love.[11]

'Church' without love is, of course, nothing of the kind. It is a woeful misnomer, a tragic anomaly. If a building bears a sign with the word 'restaurant', but has no food on offer, it is not a restaurant.

---

11. 1 Corinthians 13:1–3 (MSG).

A bank without money is not really a bank. Without love, services of 'worship' centred on the communal singing of hymns and songs become little more than pious karaoke. 'Fellowship' that is empty of love bears no resemblance to the radical, self-giving, love-impregnated *koinonia* discussed in Chapter 3. When love is absent, 'outreach' becomes nothing more than a religious recruitment drive. The most critical indictment of a church congregation is not a deficiency of faith, nor an inadequacy of knowledge. It is a failure to respond to the love of Christ in ways that create loving relationships among believers and loving behaviour towards all.

Grace in reverse

When investigating complex matters, even the evidence of well-designed studies does not provide simple answers. However, the findings of research do provide a basis for careful reflection, from which understanding can grow. Following the *Faith journeys beyond the congregations* and *Investigating the invisible church* studies a number of small focus groups reflected on the findings, and one insight which emerged from that process was the relevance of Dr Frank Lake's ideas regarding the dynamics by which love is sometimes fostered and at other times is diminished.[12] Through his work as a clinical psychologist, Lake was convinced of vital roles of acceptance, sustenance, status and achievement in attaining long-term well-being. As a theologian, he recognised these basic needs in the gospel accounts of the life of Jesus and in the teaching of the New Testament. Lake observed that there are contexts in which people feel that their worth or significance is directly related to their level of achievement. The short-term consequences of such a perspective can be a striving for better performance, generally seen as a positive trait. However, in the longer term, the impossibility of continually achieving more means that, sooner or later, attainment will decline, with a consequent loss of status and sense of rejection.

---

12. Lake, F., 1986, *Clinical theology: A theological and psychological basis to clinical pastoral care*, London: Darton, Longman & Todd.

Lake developed a model he termed 'the dynamic cycle'. Based on the life of Christ, this is entirely opposite to the progression described above. Sometimes called the 'cycle of grace', this rejects the idea that meaning in life flows out of achievement. Rather, Lake postulated, before we can achieve, we need to feel accepted. Acceptance then enables us to be nourished and sustained, and from that our sense of status develops. This solid foundation of acceptance, sustenance and status then gives rise to achievements that are not based on a need to be accepted, but that come from knowing that we are accepted. As a pioneer of pastoral counselling, Lake recognised that many difficulties in behaviour and relationships stem from a sense of not being accepted and the insecurity that generates.

When our mode of living follows the direction of the cycle of grace, affirmation and sustenance are seen as 'inputs'. For the Christian, these come from our recognition that we are loved by God and our experience of drawing inspiration and strength from him. Status and achievement are secondary 'outputs' and are the fruit of the acceptance and enabling that faith in God affords. When the cycle is reversed, it becomes a 'cycle of grief' or 'cycle of works', and the necessary inputs are understood as outputs and vice versa. So, in that distorted and ultimately destructive modus operandi, status and achievement are viewed as requisite inputs in order to gain affirmation and sustenance.

Lake saw a clear parallel between the cycle of grace and the Christian teaching regarding justification by faith. While the maxim of the reformation was *sola fide* (Latin for 'by faith alone'), prominent reformers were keen to emphasise that, while we are justified by faith alone, the faith that justifies is never alone. They stressed that the same faith that leads to forgiveness and reconciliation with God also gives rise to loving actions, prompted and energised by the grace that we ourselves have experienced.

In terms of Lake's model, having found our acceptance and sustenance in God, we are compelled by gratitude to 'Live a life filled with love, following the example of Christ'[13] and to 'love

---

13. Ephesians 5:2.

one another' *as Jesus loved us*.[14] Thus a healthy congregation is characterised by a 'cycle of grace', rooted in the knowledge that 'he loved us first'[15] and leading to an outpouring of love to others. Sadly, the cycle sometimes goes into reverse, as status and achievement are allowed to dominate – sometimes through a dynamic that we shall explore now.

The good is the enemy of the best

Christian people, while wholeheartedly affirming the truth of 'by faith alone' and the wisdom of the principles in Lake's model, nonetheless find themselves battling against influences and expectations which threaten to impose ways of understanding and manners of living that reverse the cycle of grace. For many, involvement in a local church strengthens them in that struggle and keeps the cycle of grace turning. However, what the accounts of numerous churchless Christians reveal is that some congregations, despite written creeds and genuine intentions to the contrary, become environments that are love-stifling rather than love-promoting.

Now I don't believe for a moment that there are churches that do not subscribe, in theory at least, to the importance of love. However, it does seem that, sometimes, perhaps in the genuine and well-intentioned emphasising of other aspects of Christian faith and living, love loses its rightful place of pre-eminence. When the 'best of all'[16] is diluted or superseded by other concerns (regardless of how legitimate these may be), then the way is opened for a dysfunctional, love-deficient culture to develop. In such a context, love becomes a noun that applies to everyone in general, but nobody in particular – rather than a verb that is worked out in relationships and actions with specific people. Structures and programmes that are established to serve other concerns may not be the best for facilitating loving relationships within the congregation and

---

14. John 15:12.
15. 1 John 4:19.
16. 1 Corinthians 12:31.

beyond. Love may be sincere, but it quickly becomes superficial when it is denied its rightful priority.

The lowest priorities on your to-do list are unlikely to divert attention from the matter that you deem *most* important. Rather, the real enemy of the absolutely imperative is the next most important; the most likely diversion from the top priority are the second and third priorities. The good is the enemy of the best. In church congregations there is no agenda of hatred that threatens to subvert the call to love one another. Rather, there are a number of good and important concerns that are in danger of being over-emphasised. Interlaced with accounts of unloving attitudes and behaviour in the interview transcripts of people who have disengaged from church are found stories of how matters that are central to the Christian faith were pursued with such vigour that love became sidelined.

If we look again at Paul's warning to the Corinthians, it is striking that the things that are highlighted as futile without love are, in and of themselves, good; they are godly and worthy aspirations:

If I speak with human eloquence and angelic ecstasy but don't love, I'm nothing but the creaking of a rusty gate. If I speak God's Word with power, revealing all his mysteries and making everything plain as day, and if I have faith that says to a mountain, 'Jump', and it jumps, but I don't love, I'm nothing. If I give everything I own to the poor and even go to the stake to be burned as a martyr, but I don't love, I've gotten nowhere. So, no matter what I say, what I believe, and what I do, I'm bankrupt without love.[17]

This is not a catalogue of evils or vices. Rather, Paul warns against religious experiences, powerful preaching, extraordinary acts of faith and sacrificial giving, which are rendered irritating and pointless by a lack of love. As in Corinth, so the evidence of people who have moved away from church congregations points to good things which become caustic or sour by pursuing them at the expense of loving relationships. For example, one young man spoke of how a particular 'manifestation of the Spirit' experienced

17. 1 Corinthians 13:1–3 (MSG).

by some within the congregation became an expectation for all. As a result he was left feeling 'second-rate and a bit of an outsider – it wasn't that I didn't believe or didn't want that, but I found it difficult to have the experiences'. In a similar vein, one elderly woman described how a community project, something which she was enthusiastically supportive of and viewed positively, was pursued with such single-minded passion by the leadership team that it 'sucked all the energy and resources from everything else' and 'those who were less fully involved were left feeling left on the sidelines'. An elderly man who did not get involved with the congregation's building project because of other commitments, felt 'to some extent kept at arms' length' and found that 'some horrible things were said and done in the name of the renovation project – not to me, necessarily, but it became very unpleasant for a while'.

These and other examples remind us that potentially constructive, even God-inspired activities, unless they are implemented through relationships of love, have the possibility to be harmful and even destructive. Fortunately Paul goes on to provide a valuable help, an inventory against which to check our motives, attitudes and behaviour. In the Western world, the exquisite and stirring prose of 1 Corinthians 13:4–7 is the most popular scripture reading for wedding ceremonies and has been dubbed 'the hymn of love'. However, it is good to recall its context. Paul penned these words not as a sentimental celebration, but in response to the accounts that had reached him of good gifts being abused, impatience within the family of faith and powerful but poisonous motives such as pride, envy and self-interest subverting the way of love:

Love is patient and kind. Love is not jealous or boastful or proud or rude. It does not demand its own way. It is not irritable, and it keeps no record of being wronged. It does not rejoice about injustice but rejoices whenever the truth wins out. Love never gives up, never loses faith, is always hopeful, and endures through every circumstance.[18]

---

18. 1 Corinthians 13:4–7.

The 'Great Omission'

It all seems so reasonable. Of course our lives in Christ need to reflect his character in ever-increasing measure; our lives together should demonstrate our obedience to his 'one another' commands. However, regardless of the depth and sincerity of our commitment, we cannot conjure up greater love by our own will or effort. At times Christ's aspiration for his church seems unattainable; it's just too hard. Fortunately, divine resources are on our side. Alone we cannot change, 'but the fruit of the Spirit is love'.[19] Former Archbishop William Temple used to remind people that our recognition of our own inability to summon up greater reserves of love should drive us back to its ultimate and superabundant source:

> It is no good giving me a play like Hamlet and telling me to write a play like that. Shakespeare could do it; I can't. And it is no good showing me a life like the life of Jesus and telling me to live a life like that. Jesus could do it; I can't. But if the genius of Shakespeare could come and live in me, then I could write plays like his. And if the Spirit of Christ could come into me, then I could live a life like His.[20]

It is as we allow Christ's Spirit ever-greater reign in our lives that the truth of Paul's assertion in his letter to the church in Rome becomes reality in our lives: 'God's love has been poured out into our hearts through the Holy Spirit'.[21] It is that love, cultivated through the formative endeavours often termed 'discipleship', that enables us to love 'not in word or talk but in deed and in truth'.[22] The activities we undertake in our desire to grow in love, not least prayer and allowing scripture to challenge and change us, nurture and grow God's love within us; they don't earn it. Indeed, it is in a place of humility and vulnerability that love thrives. As we

---

19. Galatians 5:22.
20. Quoted in Stott, J., 1994, *Basic Christianity*, Leicester: IVP, p. 102.
21. Romans 5:5.
22. 1 John 3:18.

realise our own inability to love and admit our brokenness, so we discover ourselves 'beloved of God', and in knowing ourselves loved become those with whom others can share their own vulnerabilities and find God loving them through us.[23]

Christian people are called to be 'disciples', a word which means learners or students. As such we are *apprenticed* to the one who 'so loved the world that he gave his one and only Son'.[24] We follow and learn from Jesus who, 'Having loved his own who were in the world, he loved them to the end'.[25] To grow as a Christian is, crucially, to grow in love. Churches are not only to be marked and motivated by love, they are also to foster love in the lives of believers. Having surveyed 430 post-congregational and non-congregational Christians, the *Investigating the invisible church* study concluded that:

> Whether Christians are part of a congregation or not, it is important that faith is nurtured and worked out in the realities of daily life. It is clear that many of those who are not engaged with a congregation are serious about developing habits that sustain and grow their Christian lives, such as prayer, scripture reading and meeting with other Christians. Congregations need to re-evaluate the opportunities they provide for Christians to explore faith, work through questions and doubts, and grow in Christian character. It is clear that, for many, the congregation alone has not provided a helpful context for discipleship.

The findings of that survey challenge the church to discover again the priority of discipleship and move beyond a predominantly educational interpretation of Jesus' final command to 'make disciples'. The fact that a quarter of respondents found the congregational environment 'superficial' and a third indicated that congregational involvement had not helped their Christian growth, reinforces the view that this aspect of the Great Commission is

---

23. For a powerful exploration of these themes, I wholeheartedly recommend Nouwen, H., 2002, *Life of the beloved*, New York: Crossroad.
24. John 3:16.
25. John 13:1.

indeed a 'Great Omission'.[26] If further confirmation of the urgency and importance of reimagining and reinvigorating discipleship were needed, *The Church Leaving Applied Research Project*[27] in England and Wales found that 37 per cent of those under 20 and 23 per cent of those over 20 agreed that 'The church was no longer helping me grow'. Similarly, Jamieson's research in New Zealand, presented in *A churchless faith*, concluded that the congregations his interviewees had experienced tended to emphasise introducing people to the Christian life but then to neglect equipping them for the journey upon which they have embarked.[28]

The contention that John underscored so emphatically in his epistles of nearly two millennia ago is that to grow as a Christian is always to grow in love. Whether Christians are engaged with a church congregation or find fellowship and accountability in other less formal ways, there is a need to rediscover the age-old disciplines of Christian formation, to re-imagine them and to ensure their outworking in daily life.[29] As the love of Christ matures within believers, as our security is anchored increasingly firmly in an enduring awareness of his love for us, we become unafraid to love others, regardless of the most profound differences.

26. Willard, D., 2014, *The great omission: Reclaiming Jesus's essential teachings on discipleship*, San Francisco, CA: HarperOne.

27. Richter, P. and Francis, L. J., 1998, *Gone but not forgotten: Church-leaving and returning*, London: Darton, Longman & Todd.

28. Jamieson, A., 2002, *A churchless faith*, London: SPCK, p. 146.

29. People such as Dallas Willard and Richard Foster have published extensively in this area, espousing the enduring benefits of ancient practices of engagement (such as prayer, fellowship, study and celebration) and the lesser-known practices of abstinence (such as solitude, silence and fasting). Good introductions to the practices of Christian formation are Foster, R., 2008, *The celebration of discipline: The path to spiritual growth*, London: Hodder & Stoughton; and Willard, D., 1991, *The spirit of the disciplines: Understanding how God changes lives*, San Francisco, CA: Harper. Proponents of the 'new monasticism' mentioned in the previous chapter are exploring ways of living out historic patterns of spirituality in contemporary life. An excellent overview of developments emerging in the UK through the new monastic movement is available in Cray, G., Mobsby, I. and Kennedy, A. (eds), 2010, *New monasticism as fresh expressions of church*. London: Canterbury Press.

So what?
Questions and activities
for further reflection

A primary activity of the church according to the New Testament
is to 'one-another' one another. We are to be: at peace with
each other, honouring one another above ourselves, accepting
one another, carrying one another's burdens, confessing our sins
to one another, offering hospitality to one another and, in and
through it all, supremely, loving one another. There are almost
sixty 'one another's in the New Testament, including a few things
we are *not* to do against or to one another, such as grumble, slan-
der or lie.

How does the way you practise your Christian faith facilitate
the kind of community espoused by the New Testament?

What do you think Dallas Willard meant by 'the Great Omission'?

'A quarter of respondents found the congregational environment
"superficial" and a third indicated that congregational involvement
had not helped their Christian growth.' To what extent do these survey responses reflect your own experience of church congregations?

Paul and friends wrote to the church in Thessalonica: 'may the
Lord make your love for one another and for all people grow
and overflow'. How do you cultivate love in your life? In your
experience, what practices in church congregations encourage
the development and overflow of loving relationships? And what
might stifle these?

CHAPTER 9

Co-missioned

Jesus called his followers to be with him, but also to be sent out. They were to be his apprentices *and* accomplices in his mission to instigate a new 'Kingdom', reflecting the love and holiness of God. Research among Christians who are not engaged with a church congregation reveals that, for some, their concern to be effective in that mission was instrumental in deciding to move out, or remain out, of congregational life. As this chapter reveals, others are finding faith through the witness of such people.

WE ARE SAFE HERE

That Sunday evening the disciples were meeting behind locked doors because they were afraid of the Jewish leaders. Suddenly, Jesus was standing there among them! 'Peace be with you,' he said. As he spoke, he showed them the wounds in his hands and his side. They were filled with joy when they saw the Lord! Again he said, 'Peace be with you. As the Father has sent me, so I am sending you.' Then he breathed on them and said, 'Receive the Holy Spirit.'

John 20:19–22

To follow Jesus is to be sent

What comes to mind when you hear the words 'mission' or 'missionary'? For many people these are words loaded with misunderstandings. Traditional images tend to emphasise extremes: cartoons of white men in pith helmets, large black Bible in hand, 'taking Jesus' to 'cannibalistic' tribes in distant and 'dark' lands – or perhaps being boiled in a large pot for their troubles! For people in the West, especially those of us in the UK, impressions of mission can be more tainted by associations with Empire, than shaped by the vision of Kingdom espoused by Jesus. Other common connotations involve celebrity evangelists preaching to multitudes and serious individuals going door-to-door.

In truth the word 'mission', rooted in the Latin word *missio*, simply means 'sending'. It's a word that does not appear in the Bible, but rather like the word 'trinity' (also absent from the Bible), it was coined to express a concept which is conveyed in the Bible. For many Christians, their notion of mission stems primarily from Jesus' instruction to his disciples to 'go and make disciples of all the nations'.[1] However, important as that Great Commission is, mission is much more than obedience to a single command. It is a thread running from Genesis to Revelation, firmly rooted in the

---

1. Matthew 28:19.

character of God. He is a 'sending God'. As one prominent Bible scholar expressed, 'If I were asked to select a text for a sermon on mission, I would have to choose the whole Bible!'[2]

In the very opening passage of the Bible we read of God *sending* forth his creative and life-giving Word. Then throughout the Hebrew Scriptures we find the Creator *sending* a family on a journey of faith in order to bless all the families of the earth.[3] From that family a people emerge, characterised by their covenant relationship with Yahweh,[4] and are sent (or 'missioned') into the world as a light to others, witnesses to the goodness of God: 'I will make you a light to the Gentiles, and you will bring my salvation to the ends of the earth.'[5]

Ultimately, of course, as we read on into the New Testament, we discover that, so deep is the love of God for his whole creation, he sent his own son. Then, as Jesus finds committed followers, he calls them to 'be with him and to be sent out';[6] these disciples ('apprentices') are also going to be apostles (meaning 'sent from'). In order to empower and enable those he co-missioned ('sent with'), God sends his Spirit. In a profound sense, all we need to know about mission is encapsulated in the words that the resurrected Jesus uttered as he spoke to a band of terrified (and then overjoyed) disciples: 'As the Father has sent me, so I am sending you.'[7] Huddled 'behind locked doors because they were afraid',[8] Jesus blessed them with peace and sent them out, beyond their self-constructed barricades.

When we wonder about the nature of mission, about the purpose and practicalities of our 'sentness', we need to dig deeper into the mind-blowing implications of Jesus' words. What does

---

2. John Stott, witnessed by the author as part of an address at All Nations Christian College, Ware in 1993.

3. Genesis 12:1–3.

4. 'Yahweh' is the pronunciation of the transliteration YHWH most widely accepted by Hebrew scholars.

5. Isaiah 49:6.

6. Mark 3:14.

7. John 20:21.

8. John 20:19.

it mean to be sent 'as he was sent'? To answer that question and to allow the consequences to direct and shape our choices is the labour of a lifetime. However, before we explore what any of this has to do with Christians who are disengaged from congregational expressions of church, let's look at how the apostles are likely to have understood their involvement in God's mission from reflecting on those words 'As the Father has sent me . . .'.

Flesh and blood

The word 'incarnation' is a theological jargon word that we associate with the events of the first Christmas. However, when we break it down, it is not as foreign or technical as it first sounds. It has its roots in that word 'carne' as in chilli con *carne*, which literally translates as chilli with meat (or flesh). Or as in *carnivore*, meaning flesh eating. So when God took on *flesh* and came into our world in the person of Jesus, he was *incarnated*. As Paul explained, 'Though he was God, he did not think of equality with God as something to cling to. Instead, he gave up his divine privileges; he took the humble position of a slave and was born as a human being.'[9] Jesus fully *em-bodied* the life and character of God, becoming 'the visible image of the invisible God'.[10] A contemporary translation of the opening phrases of John's Gospel captures the awe, reverence and wonder evoked from grappling with this truth: 'The Word became flesh and blood, and moved into the neighbourhood. We saw the glory with our own eyes, the one-of-a-kind glory, like Father, like Son, generous inside and out, true from start to finish.'[11]

Clearly, in saying to his followers, 'As the Father sent me, so I am sending you', Jesus was fully aware that they could never personify the life and character of God in the unique way that he did. However, he did see their vocation as a continuation of

---

9. Philippians 2:6–7.
10. Colossians 1:15.
11. John 1:14 (MSG).

his own: 'I tell you the truth, anyone who believes in me will do the same works I have done.'[12] Their joint calling to holiness, to exemplify godly values and to 'go' and be with people, is articulated in Jesus' solemn prayer for them (and for us)[13] to be *in* the world but not *of* the world.[14] As his apprentices, they were to allow all that he taught and showed them to transform them and they were to go, to be in proximity with people of other values and other beliefs, to eschew the temptation to construct a cosy compound or to hunker down in a religious ghetto. Thus, they were (and we are) to be *incarnational*, living the life of God in the everyday and the commonplace.

Ultimately, mission is what God is doing in the world. It is not the 'mission of the church' or of any parachurch or 'mission' agency; it is God's initiative to liberate and restore his creation. And yet, astonishingly, he calls us to be his accomplices. As former Archbishop Rowan Williams explained – with beguiling, almost childlike simplicity – mission, from a human perspective, is 'finding out what God is doing and joining in'.[15] It is more than following the example of Jesus; it is walking in step with what he is doing now.

Fears of leakage

Once my interest in the increasing number of Christians disengaged from congregational Christianity was piqued, I soon devoured the few books I could find on the subject. Within that

---

12. John 14:12.

13. It is always humbling and encouraging to remember that Jesus had us in mind as he prayed for those closest to him: 'I am praying not only for these disciples but also for all who will ever believe in me through their message' (John 17:20).

14. John 17:6–19.

15. Archbishop's Presidential Address – General Synod, York, July 2003 – See more at: http://rowanwilliams.archbishopofcanterbury.org/articles.php /1826/archbishops-presidential-address-general-synod-york-july-2003#sthash .Uq1vnsao.dpuf.

limited literature, there often seemed to be a subtext of fear which saw the 'haemorrhaging' of believers from congregations as a substantial threat to the missionary endeavour of the Christian community. In Michael Fanstone's *The sheep that got away*, the move away from congregations by believers is portrayed as a catastrophe, which is tragic for the leavers, heart-breaking for God, disastrous for the congregations and undermining of mission. The clear premise underlying the author's survey of church-leavers was that less church-going equates to weakened Christian influence within local communities and wider society.

Fanstone's respondents were asked to indicate their experience from a list of possible explanations for discontinuing the habit of church-going. If you have paid attention to the previous chapters of this book, you will be unsurprised to discover that the reasons selected by those surveyed indicated that church-leavers found the congregational experience irrelevant to everyday life, boring, and they felt they did not belong. In fact these were considerably more prevalent answers than any of the others on offer.

Apart from asking what these people did on Sundays, no line of enquiry in that survey probed their practice of the Christian faith or their vision for mission. These people were viewed as 'leakage'[16] from congregations; the unstated assumption was that, like precious liquid spilled from its legitimate container, they were spoiled and making no further worthwhile contribution to God's purposes. In terms of Jesus' analogies, rather than being salt in the world, adding flavour and halting decay, they were perceived as those who had 'lost their saltiness . . . trampled underfoot as worthless'.[17]

When I published an article in local newspapers about my plan to conduct research among Christians who did not attend church, in addition to the responses from people who identified themselves as fitting my criteria, there were others from individuals who were uneasy and unhappy about my proposal. They were

---

16. Fanstone, M. J., 1993, *The sheep that got away*, Oxford: Monarch, pp. 23 and 28.
17. Matthew 5:13–16.

anxious that, by undertaking such a study, I was 'legitimising [the] rebellion' of church-leavers. One correspondent claimed that I was 'devaluing the word "Christian" and undermining [his] own witness'. Another email implored me to 'remember the urgent sense of belonging to each other in the Body of Christ' which characterised the early Church, something which the writer saw as 'essential to our faith, and [offering] us something distinctive to offer the world'. The person concluded, 'I believe this is the way to win souls back for Christ, rather than merging in with run-of-the-mill values and becoming basically a folk religion.'

To be honest, I had much sympathy with the accusations levelled at me. Those who expressed apprehension at what I was doing were obviously passionate and well-intentioned. However, the truth is that I was simply trying to understand an undeniable reality. The people I was contacting did not need to be 'won back to Christ' and did not want to be 'enlightened of the indispensable benefits of fellowship'. Thankfully, through correspondence and conversations, most of those who shared their reservations and objections came to be supportive of the project.

When viewed through a lens that has been shaped and tinted by a solely congregation-centric view of mission, church-leaving and any form of Christianity that is practised beyond the congregational context are causes for heartache and anguish. Previous studies did not recognise and document 'missional concern' as a motive for church-leaving, because surveys did not ask questions related to this possibility. When non-congregational believers are assumed to be anomalous and, without doubt, on a slippery and precipitous path that could only lead to a shrunken faith or to apostasy, it is inevitable that the focus of research is on why they left and whether they will return.

Unexpectedly, when, as part of the *Faith journeys beyond the congregations* study, people were invited simply to tell their own story without constraint or direction, a sense of commitment to participate in God's mission was prominent in more than half of their accounts. While most people described some negative experiences that acted as push factors, a majority of interviewees implied that, on balance, it was a concern for the missional challenges in their area that was a decisive motivator for their disengagement from the congregation. They explained that what they perceived as mission opportunities were inadequately met or, in some cases, not taken seriously, by the local congregation.

For several of the churchless Christians we listened to, closely linked to this concern for mission was the issue discussed in Chapter 6 – that life as a member of the congregation demanded more and more time to be spent on internal matters, leaving less time to relate to others beyond the Christian community. You may remember the explanation of the person quoted there, who recalled how growing demands to be on committees and involved in 'keeping things going' seemed to 'snowball' and become 'all-consuming':

As we got to the end of the 90s, what was really striking us were two things – time is short, years are passing quickly, this commission that we have to be active in the world as ambassadors for Christ was something that was much more theoretical than practical it seemed.

Having failed to convince those in leadership to address the issue, this person and their spouse decided to leave the congregation. Despite sadness at having failed to communicate their vision to the minister, Elders and wider congregation, they were immediately encouraged by how the time that previously had been used in church-related matters was used in engaging with others beyond the Christian community:

It was like getting an eighth day to the week. It was unbelievable what sort of opened up. Our opportunities to be impactful are just on another scale completely. We talk with lots more people than we ever did outside the faith community about our life in faith. We get asked a lot more than we ever did before about serious stuff of life from people who are themselves in positions of responsibility and dealing with all kinds of complexities and uncertainties and ambiguities that they face perhaps in their careers but as much in the family or in their relationships.

Applying metaphors such as 'leakage' and 'haemorrhage' to church-leaving evokes images of some kind of ecclesiastical incontinence or slow death by blood loss. More seriously, these analogies fail to recognise the life and witness of Christians beyond the congregation, implying that their only contribution was church-going. Paradoxically, the fear that declining church rolls and growing numbers of Christians beyond the congregations dilute the missional impact of congregations is a mirror image of the concerns expressed by many who have left. The evidence of recent studies suggests that it is a disappointment about the ineffective missional influence of the congregation and an impulse to explore alternatives that explain why some church-leavers have disengaged from traditional congregational life.

Data from surveys adds further support to the finding that Christians who are outside the congregational setting often recognise the importance of mission and are well motivated to share their faith with others. The *Investigating the invisible church* survey, because the questions were based on the themes that emerged from the kinds of interviews quoted above, included questions related to missional concern. Of those whose HIRS scores (see Chapter 3) indicated high levels of commitment to the Christian faith, 82 per cent agreed with the statement, 'The world needs to hear the teaching of Jesus Christ', compared with 34 per cent of those with scores below thirty. In response to a negatively worded partner statement, 'The teaching of Jesus Christ has nothing to say to the modern world', 87 per cent of the high scorers disagreed and 57 per cent of this same cohort also indicated that they 'occasionally talk to friends and neighbours about faith'.

Out of the salt cellar

When most people think of 'church' they imagine an assembly of people gathering for the purpose of shared worship. However, most of the time, Christians, even the most committed members of congregations, are not congregated with other believers; they are at home, at work, at school, engaged in social and leisure activities. Here, then, are two distinct modes of being of the Christian community: gathered and dispersed. At different times in the history of the Church (and in different parts of the world and within different church traditions) one modus operandi has tended to be emphasised more than the other. For many traditional churches in the Western world, this second way of being, 'the church dispersed', despite occupying by far the majority of the believers' time, is something of a blind spot.

One interviewee in the *Faith journeys beyond the congregations* study described a moment of insight when, one Sunday morning, at a time when he would usually have been heading for church (gathered), he encountered a neighbour. I'll let him tell you in his own words:

I was planning on going to [name of church] and I checked my emails and there was an email from the minister saying 'we need somebody to lead the singing this morning, so if anybody out there is keen to help we'd be glad to hear from them'. And my immediate impulse was 'OK Lord, sounds like a change of plan', so I reached for my Psalm book and two things happened spontaneously, or simultaneously: one was the thought 'if you jump every time you're asked, you'll never be done jumping'. That was new to me. I didn't feel that was me speaking. The other was a children's song . . . that I hadn't heard in about a dozen years or more, that went 'Are you a good neighbour? Are you too much in a hurry to care for the stranger, will you walk on the other side?' OK, I didn't expect that!

So I was talking to God and said, 'Lord, you know the connotations of these things in my head, and I don't want to just go off on a whim, but I'm going out to the car to get my jacket and if something happens between here and there I take it you don't want me to go to [name of church] this morning, or necessarily anywhere else.' I went out to the car, put my hand on my jacket and a voice said '[name of interviewee]! Come and watch me jump on my trampoline'. That I really didn't expect! I expected a crisis, I expected somebody who was going to need help.

I wasn't specific. But it was enough of an answer to think 'OK, let's run with this'. So, [name of child], two doors along was bouncing on his trampoline . . . and so I said 'very good'. And then his Dad came out and we blethered – we knew each other, not that well, but well enough to have a conversation – and he talked and he talked for ages, and then his wife came out and she talked, and then eventually they had to go somewhere and as I was leaving their garden another neighbour came along and I had another conversation, and for three hours there was conversation after conversation after conversation, and it wasn't about deep, meaningful spiritual stuff but I felt 'this is important, God's said "listen to what's going on here"'. I felt suddenly struck by the fact that Sunday, at that time, was a different day to Saturday for a lot of these neighbours. Saturday was the day they got stuff done, they'd go shopping, they'd hang out, particularly Sunday morning, and I had been clueless to that because I was so full of the Sunday pantomime!

The structure of our Sunday was pretty full . . . I was completely unaware of the fact that people had time to sit and talk. So, from that point on, probably for the next year, most Sunday mornings I was often sitting out in the Square rather than in church, and there were a number of significant conversations that spoke volumes to me – partly because these people wouldn't have taken those questions to the church – they didn't – but I became a familiar enough figure that they would talk and I felt there was something important for me to learn in that process.

I have been extravagant in quoting this transcript at length because it highlights the concern expressed by many people throughout that study regarding the two 'modes of operation' of the Church/Christian community. There is the church 'gathered' and there is the church 'scattered' and, according to many of our interviewees, the time spent in gathering mode can leave little time or energy for the opportunities for engaging with those beyond the church walls. Not only that, but, according to some, the activities of gathered church did little to equip them for most of life.

To return to the analogy used by Jesus, it seems that congregations sometimes emphasise the salt's role in filling the salt cellar rather than facilitating its dispersal and ensuring the widespread benefit of its seasoning and disinfecting properties.

When the seed falls beyond the Christian bubble

In addition to people who have founded informal gatherings almost inadvertently, there are others whose ardent vision for mission leads them to actively explore alternative ways of being church. One married couple in the *Faith journeys beyond the congregations* study described how their frustration with the lack of missional understanding and effectiveness of congregations they experienced led them into initiating a non-congregational expression of church. Through leading home-based evangelistic courses in their home, a number of people embraced the Christian faith. However, they found it necessary to create additional opportunities to bridge the cultural gap between the course and the congregation:

> For about two years and within that context we made disciples, not through the main church meetings, but initially through a [name of course], and then we spoke with the leadership and they agreed that we continue to meet with these people. It was still within the framework of the church structure, but it was quite a different dynamic really from the main church meetings.

Through the experience of running several such courses and supporting those who committed themselves to the Christian faith, they became convinced that they needed to be part of a different kind of church. While the leaders of the congregation were delighted that people with no previous church experience were finding faith, there seemed to be no willingness to adapt congregational life to meet the needs of those people:

> After about two years we really had a different way of seeing things. It was the issue of 'how do you incorporate people from

a non-Christian background into an established church?' It was that – it was the difficulty of passing through those cultural barriers for the recent convert, the person who had recently made a commitment to Christ. That perhaps was primary in our thinking for the moving on. And so we moved on in peace, there was no personal fall-out or acrimony or bitterness, and we went to a larger church in the town . . . And we met there for three or four years . . . In a sense, although we were in the heart of the church, we weren't perhaps closely associated with some of the programme – rather we found that we could use our home and we could use meals to make disciples . . . during those years we reflected on our Christian life and we reflected on what aspects of service had cultivated most development in our own lives and also in the lives of the people that we were working with. Of course, that also made us reflect on what were the things that required a lot of effort, that perhaps had not been particularly fruitful, either for ourselves or for the people that we sought to love and whom we sought to nurture in the Christian faith.

Having decided to disengage from congregational life, their gathering with other Christians and with people exploring faith is centred on a rhythm of shared meals, walks and the conversation that these enable:

Our focus is on relationship, and we do that through meals and we walk with people. There may be better ways but I don't yet know of better ways of spending time with people than eating and drinking with them, and walking with them. I see this as the strategy the Lord Jesus used . . . we meet together and we follow what I believe to be the simplicity of the church in the New Testament. And so we don't have a religious building, we don't have any plan to have a religious building. If we grew – and we have been growing – we would multiply into various homes or other places where we could meet, and we're praying for that. We've got the beginnings of a second group that started over the last month or two.

One of the pleasant surprises of the research that began in the Highlands and Islands, an area where I thought I had a thorough grasp of the church scene, was encountering exceptionally committed people involved in a variety of non-congregational forms of church. As one such person explained:

I think that fellowships like the one we have here in the home tend to pass below the radar. Such fellowships often don't have denominational links, they don't have obvious religious buildings on a street corner, they tend not to have church announcements in the local paper and so, although quite a number of such groups do exist in the [name of town] area, they probably pass below the radar.

Echoes of eras past

It may seem bizarre to hear of people leaving church out of a desire to be more missionally effective, but it is a contemporary reality. And there's more, because those with eyes to see will recognise it as part of a recurring pattern down through the ages. Throughout much of the history of the Christian movement the Church existed in two distinct structures or forms. One was the locally rooted, stable, congregation that has become the default position of Western Christianity. This model of being church developed out of the synagogue pattern of the first century. Drawing together both genders and every generation means that there is a degree of biological perpetuation. By creating a distinct community, characterised by the fruit of the Spirit, people outside the circle of believers are attracted, welcomed, instructed in the faith and assimilated.

So far, so familiar. Nothing unusual there. The names of present-day churches often intimate their local focus: Boat-of-Insh Free Church, Beddington Parish Church, Clwydfro Methodist Chapel and so forth. But the frustration or disappointment that we sometimes hear from Christians who reside outside this kind of system reminds us that this is not the whole story. Throughout most of its history the Church has exhibited another mode of being. Equally 'church', but characterised by a mobile, flexible, highly committed team with specific purposes beyond a particular local community.

The late Professor Ralph Winter authored a detailed history of 'The two structures of God's redemptive mission'[18] in which he explains how various forms of monastic tradition began early in the life of the Church. He goes on to describe how, until the Protestant Reformation, the Church comprised these two distinctive but synergetic ways of being: the default stable congregation (which he calls 'modal': committed to pastoring, teaching, caring, and nurturing faith) and what he refers to as the 'sodal', which emphasised sending and pioneering. While the modern perception of monks as people who 'fled the world' has some limited basis in fact, the original expansion of Christianity across Europe was not led by vicars, ministers or congregations 'with a vision for outreach'; Europe became Christian through the labours and witness of monks.[19]

Could it be that one cause of the exasperation or disappointment that sometimes leads people with a particular missional concern out of congregations is the lack of legitimate pioneering structures that parallel the role of monastic movements of the past? I'm not suggesting that all such people become nuns or monks! And you may say that there is a multitude of mission agencies and parachurch organisations for those who feel the urge to pioneer something beyond the congregation. However, the significant difference between the sodal structures of the past and contemporary parachurch entities is that the former were understood as authentic expressions of church.

George Lings, Director of the Church Army's Research Unit, who has extensive experience of pioneering movements in the Anglican

---

18. Winter, R., 2013, *Foundations of the World Christian Movement: A larger perspective*, Pasadena, CA: William Carey International University Press, pp. 227–36.

19. Ian Adam quotes Bishop Stephen Cotterell as stating this and suggesting that, by implication, mission movements need to root themselves in similar patterns of wisdom and practice in Cray, G., Mobsby, I. and Kennedy, A. (eds), 2010, *New monasticism as fresh expressions of church*, London: Canterbury Press, p. 37.

context, suggests that it is a lack of awareness of these two dimensions of church and a failure of denominations to apply the lessons of the past that result in pioneers 'frustrated with church' and ecclesial authorities 'alarmed by pioneers'.[20] The modal has a tendency towards risk aversion; the sodal a predisposition for risk taking.

History seems to suggest that when the sodal is muted, missional energy is dissipated or hindered, and God plants the vision to reassert the sodal dimension of church. After all both modes are instincts that naturally arise from following Christ. It is inevitable that both are deeply rooted in the DNA of the Church because Jesus, as head of the Church,[21] is both pastor and pioneer.[22]

Most of the overseas mission enterprises of the nineteenth century were initiated by organisations which were independent of mainstream church authorities. The same can be said of, for example, the Salvation Army, as it arose from its Methodist origins. Leading mission historian, Professor Andrew Walls, goes as far as suggesting that God seems to raise up sodal groups and organisations not merely out of his creativity and missionary heart, but also at times when the mainstream (modal) church is weak, ailing and, humanly speaking, confronting its possible demise. However, there is also an opposite tendency at work. A study of pioneering movements of the past also shows the tendency for them to be subsumed into the modal. Winter's historical account notes a 'centralizing perspective' of denominational leaders, 'especially Presbyterians', whereby pioneering structures, previously merely 'related' to denominations, gradually became 'dominated' by them.[23]

---

20. The 2014 version of George Lings' talk, 'Why modality and sodality thinking is vital to understand future church', can be found here: www.churcharmy.org.uk/Publisher/File.aspx?ID=138339.

21. Ephesians 1:22–23.

22. See John 10:14 and Hebrews 12:2.

23. Winter, *Foundations of the World Christian Movement*, p. 228.

The fact that some people feel the need to escape the Christian bubble does not necessarily suggest a shortcoming of a congregation; neither does it point to a lack of commitment or unwillingness to persevere on the part of the leaver. When Christians leave churches, most of them don't leave the Church – and when they leave churches out of an earnest desire to respond to Christ's call to go, they are not deserters of the modal, they are reminders of its rightful and complementary alter ego. The genuinely sodal, with all its pioneering energy and vision, is a gift to the Church and a gift to the world.

For most people in the Western world of the twenty-first century, Christianity is synonymous with church in its modal role. However, both empirical evidence and the story of Christianity's development suggest that a synthesis of modal and sodal, two forms of the one Church, fosters missional impact; the modal builds bridges and the sodal creates outposts. To deny the sodal, to dismiss it as an optional bolt-on, or to regard it as illegitimate and schismatic is rather like hobbling a horse, where the attaching of constraints to its legs hampers movement and impedes progress. Once again, here is an invitation to the Church, not to innovate something radically new, but to rediscover an aspect of its rich heritage and to re-imagine its application in the contemporary world.

So what?
Questions and activities
for further reflection

Are your own natural inclinations most comfortable with the modal expression of church – or the sodal? Why might that be?

Why do you think that, historically, it has proved impossible to retain a focus on both modes within the same organisational structures?

How do you see both modes of Christian community in action in your own context? If you don't, can you imagine what a balance of the two might look like in practice?

Do you think that new pioneering movements, such as Fresh Expressions, constitute a resurgence of the sodal aspect of church?

Perhaps the tendency of modal forms of church to subsume the sodal stems partly from a fear of risk taking and the possibility of 'things going off the rails'. What kinds of measures could protect pioneering groups from risks and assure modal groups of the legitimacy?

Reflect on the fact that the word 'radical' comes from the Latin word meaning 'rooted'. In what ways are Christians called to be radical in the contemporary sense of that word and in what ways are we required to be rooted? Are there ways in which the two are intertwined?

CHAPTER 10

Glimpses of the way ahead?

We have heard the voices of committed Christians who are no longer (or were never) part of a church congregation. Each person's story is unique, but recurring themes and common experiences have been highlighted. Having put some human flesh on the bare statistics of historic shifts in the Christian community, let's try to discern its trajectory. Where is the Church heading? In the decline of institutional forms and the rise in more organic, informal practices we detect signs of a 'rewilding' of the gospel.

THE VISIBLE CHURCH   THE INVISIBLE CHURCH

*'See, the former things have come to pass, and new things
I now declare; before they spring forth, I tell you of them.'*

Isaiah 42:9 (NRSV)

New things do I declare

Last week a friend went to buy the latest edition of a video game.
The game was being launched that very day. Usual business hours
are 8am to 10pm, but the shop had been open since midnight to
cater for the many folk who couldn't sleep for fear of awaking
to being out of date. Imagine his disappointment to discover that
they were already sold out of the particular format he needed.
After all, he was told, only a small supply of that particular version had been bought in, as not more than a handful of nostalgic
enthusiasts use such an antiquated device. He had bought it, new,
for his daughter two years ago!

It seems that, in Western societies, we are somewhat conflicted
in how we view 'the new'. On the one hand we revere and adore
it. Advertising executives would not spend millions on bombard-
ing us with far-fetched promises about the latest range of 'new
and improved' products unless they were confident of our sus-
ceptibility to the cult of the new. On one level we associate new
with good and the latest with the best. Ironically, such campaigns
are sometimes inserted into the incessant stream of television
programmes which revere and adore the old. 'Retro' is in vogue;
what seems old-fashioned or outmoded to the untrained eye is
vintage or 'a timeless classic' to others.

As we seek to discern where the future of the Church lies, it is
important to recognise that there will always be, at the core of
Christian community, the same abiding and unchanging truths
which compelled the first disciples of Christ to risk everything to
share good news with the whole world. However, what emerges
as the unchanging gospel encounters new contexts is unpredictable. While the scriptures enable us to know much about God's

character, we can never reduce him to a set of principles. He not only creat*ed* (past tense); he acts and *creates* (present tense). Although Christianity has adopted the cross as its chief symbol and the events of the crucifixion enacted at a specific time in history are absolutely central to our faith, we follow a saviour who is alive. His Spirit inspires, empowers and transforms. God 'is able, through his mighty power at work within us, to accomplish infinitely more than we might ask or think'.[1]

Isaiah's proclamation, 'the former things have come to pass, and new things I now declare' had a specific and immediate application to those who first heard him. Later generations saw in these words the promise of the Suffering Servant, the one who would open blind eyes, release captives and shed light in darkness – and understood its fulfilment in Jesus. However, in addition, these words also declare an abiding certainty: God is *always* doing a new thing. Sometimes the 'new thing' is one more subtle, understated, indiscernible movement in his sustaining of creation, shaping of circumstances and gracious provision; his 'mercies are new every morning'.[2] At other times we recognise his hand in epoch-changing events.

In terms of the fundamentals, Solomon was right to say that 'Nothing under the sun is truly new'[3] and yet the words which opened the second chapter of this book, words attributed to the same man, remind us that the wise person is not only open to new ideas, but seeks them out. If we believe that God is alive and active – and if we believe that our calling is to 'find out what God is doing and join in' – then we have a sacred responsibility to actively discern the fingerprints and footsteps of our Creator. As we look at the evidence of research among churchless Christians, what are we to conclude? And how are we to respond?

---

1. Ephesians 3:20.
2. Lamentations 3:23.
3. Ecclesiastes 1:9.

Time to collect your takeaway

Here we are in the final chapter and I am eager that, before you put this book down, you reflect on what you are going to 'take away' from it. Please pause and think about that for a moment.

I find myself wondering how you have read this book so far. If you were asked to summarise its key message, what might you say? No doubt your perspective on its contents will have been shaped by your own experiences of faith and church and your current situation. Some readers may interpret the preceding chapters as a critique of the church, which may resonate with their own perceptions or may challenge them. Many, I hope, will have heard a message of hope. Perhaps you had assumed the reliability of other researchers and writers who have understood the incontrovertible and dramatic decline in church attendance as a symptom of Western society's headlong plunge into secularism. However, having heard the stories of some of the people behind the statistics, you are now more encouraged and optimistic. If you are a Christian who is not a church-goer, you may be feeling better understood, less unusual, and part of a broader phenomenon. You may have heard, in the accounts of others and the reflections on these, ideas and explanations that help you to make sense of your own journey in faith.

From the beginning my hope has been that, through careful listening to the stories of individuals and conscientious analysis of more extensive studies, we might catch glimpses of what God is doing in and through (and in spite of) the substantial and complex shifts in the configuration of the Christian community. As a social reformer, founder of modern nursing and pioneer statistician, Florence Nightingale came to believe that 'To understand God's thoughts we must study statistics, for these are the measure of His purpose.'[4]

While, in principle, I concur with 'The Lady of the Lamp', when applied to the patterns and expressions of the Christian community, a simple extrapolation of statistics will only reveal

---

4. Everitt, B., 1999, *Chance rules: An informal guide to probability, risk, and statistics*, New York: Springer, p. 137.

present trajectories; it will not, with any degree of reliability, predict destinations. The extensive and growing body of data related to church-leavers and non-congregational faith certainly enriches our understanding of the current situation greatly. However, inferring an unknown (the future) from a known (the past) with any degree of accuracy is limited to spheres of life which demonstrate stability over time, and are, therefore, 'predictable'.

While some might argue that certain sectors of the Christian community, particularly the parish churches of the UK, display considerable constancy, it is important to remember the essence of Christian community: 'The wind blows wherever it wants. Just as you can hear the wind but can't tell where it comes from or where it is going, so you can't explain how people are born of the Spirit.'[5] Indeed, in the light of John's reminder about the mysterious ways of the Spirit, it could be argued that, in the case of church, predictability should cause concern and may even be a symptom of institutionalisation quenching the life of the Spirit.

When it comes to discerning the direction of the Church on the basis of empirical evidence, it is also necessary to ponder the caveats that history offers. The chronicles of the Christian movement remind us that, while attempts to harness, steer or exploit the Church may have stifled the life of the Spirit, it cannot be extinguished. God is God and will break through and do the unimaginable – whenever and however. In earlier chapters we have touched upon the particular events of 312 when, unexpectedly, Christians ceased to be hunted down like animals and became part of a religious community protected and favoured by the supreme mortal power of the day. And who would have imagined that, after a thousand years of the monastery dominating society in England, Wales and Ireland, in less than five years (1536 and 1541), not a single one would remain.

In these dramatic periods of intense transformation, we can, from our limited and imperfect perspective, identify both constructive consequences and undesirable outcomes. In the rise of Constantine and the Christianisation of his empire we see a merciful

---

5. John 3:8.

reprieve from harsh persecution, but also the taming of what had been a radical dissident movement. In the precipitous annihilation of British monasteries of the Dissolution we observe the liquidation of a vast apparatus of spiritual formation, Christian education and cultural patronage,[6] but also the purging of widespread corruption and the hastening of the demise of an ailing institution.

Although paradigm-shifting moments in church history can seem to arise out of nowhere, like strikes of lightning from a cloudless sky, as we see them in their context, we recognise that changes in wider society have often been the harbinger of historic makeovers of the Church. For example, there can be little doubt that the rapid development and widespread adoption of printing technology created the preconditions for the legal developments and administrative processes of the Dissolution in most of Britain – just as it played a vital role in the promotion and dissemination of ideas during the Reformation in other parts of Europe.[7]

Just as your independent financial advisor should caution you that 'Past performance is no guarantee of future results' when it comes to stocks and shares, so, as we seek to determine what the trends and tendencies examined in this book mean for the Christian movement, both theology and history offer significant caveats to any simple projection. Those who forecast the demise of particular denominations[8] and others who predict that the Church will remain on its present course until 'we intentionally

---

6. G. W. Bernard, in his history of the Suppression of the Monasteries, states that there were 900 monasteries prior to the dissolution and they owned about one third of the land of England, Wales and Ireland. Bernard, G. W., 2011, 'The dissolution of the monasteries', *History*, 96(324), pp. 390–409.

7. Edwards, M., 2004, *Printing, propaganda, and Martin Luther*, Minneapolis, MN: Augsburg Fortress Publishers.

8. Based on rates of decline in church membership and attendance at the start of the millennium, Stuart Murray observed that the Methodist Church would hit rock bottom in 2037, the Church of Scotland would be closing its last congregation in 2033 and that the Church in Wales would be unsustainable by 2020. Murray, S., 2004, *Post-Christendom: Church and mission in a strange new world*, Carlisle: Paternoster Press, p. 6.

act upon it with new paradigms'[9] misconstrue the nature of the evidence and the fundamental qualities of the Church.

The Church too is on a journey

In Chapter 7 we explored the idea, rooted in the Judeo-Christian scriptures themselves and developed by writers as diverse as the spiritual guides of Christianity's first centuries and modern-day psychologists, that the metaphor of 'journey' is powerful and helpful in understanding an individual's experience of faith. At its most simple, the journey of the believer is seen as a movement from an un-critiqued faith to a deeper and broader perspective, passing through various crises and seasons of doubt or questioning; a kind of 'pilgrim's progress' through seasons of 'orientation', 'disorientation' and 're-orientation'. While an assortment of terminology has been employed over the centuries, there is remarkable consensus that the process is iterative, with similar pathways from simplicity via times of struggle or confusion towards a peaceful reconciliation, repeated over a lifetime, but always different. What about applying the same metaphor to the Church as a whole?

Just as individual wayfarers have sensed a compelling resonance with the journey analogy, does it also offer guidance for those of us concerned to understand what has occurred, what is happening and where it all might be leading in terms of the wider Christian family? As a multiplication of 'disciple', should not 'church' demonstrate similar characteristics in its development to those of the individual Christian? As pilgrims through the ages have drawn encouragement and elicited hope from the codified experiences of saints who have travelled the road ahead, what might the same precepts suggest when related to the journeying of the wider Christian community?

---

9. Halter, H. and Smay, M., 2010, *AND: The gathered and scattered church*, Grand Rapids, MI: Zondervan, p.153.

When an ocean-going yacht cuts across the briny deep it does so on a particular bearing. While the influence of changeable winds and hidden currents may be impossible to predict with pinpoint accuracy, the direction of travel gives a reasonable idea of potential endpoints. Are there ways in which we can view the research underpinning this book as indicating the direction of travel of the Christian community? And, if so, what does that tell us about possible or probable destinations?

Now, in one vital sense, we are already well provided with metaphors for the eventual condition and status of the Church. In particular, the imagery of the 'bride of Christ' provides a potent and glorious reminder that, ultimately, the Church is the creation of the Holy Spirit and the object of Christ's love. It is the clear resolve of Jesus that, through his life, death and resurrection, he will be united with a Church which 'will be holy and without fault'.[10]

When the tragic failures of the past or the heart-rending shortcomings of the present threaten to lead us into despair, we need to recall that, even when reality seems considerably off-course, the eventual destination of 'the Lord's people' is already known. Like the forty years of wanderings of the people of Israel, our route choice may sometimes seem questionable at best, but the passage itself has a purpose and the endpoint is assured.

While taking as given the magnificent hope of the Church's eventual total union with Christ, what glimpses of our current heading are sufficiently clear to provide pointers for the immediate future and beyond? We need to evaluate our direction of travel and take steps to ensure that we are on a heading that takes us in the right direction. We need to constantly invite God to sit in the stern and rest his hand on the tiller. While taking seriously the caveats offered by history and the fact that 'God moves in mysterious ways', a few key trends can be observed which are noteworthy because of their prevalence and significance.

---

10. Ephesians 5:27.

Paradigm shift? Or something else?

The desire here is to focus on a small number of themes which emerge from reliable evidence with a degree of clarity that renders them indisputable. As an avid reader of literature related to the development of the church, I sometimes groan as yet another 'paradigm shift' is announced. This is a term which has been adulterated. It first appeared in the important book by American scientist and philosopher, Thomas Kuhn, *The structure of scientific revolutions*,[11] where it referred to a revolution in worldview. It was definitely not an idiom for the latest new idea. Rather, it expressed a change in understanding so fundamental, that it changed the landscape of some area of endeavour. An obvious example would be the upheaval that occurred when it was realised that the solar system is centred on the sun rather than the earth. Prior to the ideas of Copernicus and the evidence gathered by Galileo's telescope, it was obvious to all that the sun rose in the morning, travelled across the sky and set in the evening, as it journeyed across the sky. In time, but not without cries of 'heresy' and the persecution of those proposing the new paradigm, the previous idea was replaced with a new concept.

In that word 'replaced', lies the essence of a paradigm shift. Kuhn's purpose in coining the term was to explain what transpires when evidence is uncovered which does not fit with the universally accepted model. A paradigm shift ushers in a new way of seeing. Unfortunately, in a desire for ever greater hyperbole, the term has been overused to the point of becoming hollow. Especially in the world of business and, to some extent, in the world of church, it is a phrase that is applied to any significant change of perspective. We are told that companies where strategy is no longer forged in the boardroom, but is shaped by the customer's perspective, have undergone a paradigm shift. Posts on Christian websites and blogs proclaim 'Paradigm Shifts in the

---

11. Kuhn, T., 1962, *The structure of scientific revolutions*, Chicago, IL: University of Chicago Press.

Church' which, far from reflecting a revolution in worldview turn out to be relatively trivial or parochial.

Do the changes in the Christian community explored in this book constitute paradigm shift? This is not a matter of semantics. The question does not merely enquire whether the changes we see are widespread and significant. Rather it asks whether these changes represent a transformation so fundamental and comprehensive that the new must replace what has gone before. In the accounts of church-leavers and other Christians who have never been engaged with a traditional congregation, we not only discover a valuable and constructive critique of features of the previously dominant form of church, we also find glimpses of the shape of things to come. In reports of faith that thrives beyond congregational involvement, we find signs of hope and pointers to the Christian community of tomorrow. But paradigm shift? No!

What the evidence points to is a reshaping, rebalancing or reconfiguration of the Church. Yes, for some people their journey takes them away from church *and* from Christianity, but for most, given time, they find or develop revised ways of expressing a faith which is characterised by a high degree of continuity with the beliefs they held while engaged with church.

So, if essential beliefs and a hunger for fellowship continue to characterise much Christian life beyond congregational involvement, what does change? Weighing up all the evidence, a number of changes of emphases can be identified. While not driven by fundamental changes in understanding, together they comprise an important and substantial reshaping of the Christian community.

From institutional to organic

The word 'institution' has pejorative insinuations for some. I use it here simply to describe a high degree of organisation. There is nothing wrong with institutions per se. However, the data upon which this book is founded shows that forms of Christian community that are highly organised are declining and that most people who move away from church congregations are involved in fellowship that is informal and highly relational.

Of course even the most casual network or group demands a degree of organisation, but the difference between the traditional congregation and the alternatives that are emerging is immense. It is the difference between 'when to meet next' and a whole legal and administrative framework. It is the contrast between 'who brings the cake next time' and layers of bylaws and policies, often couched in archaic language, which only a few specialists really understand.

One simple definition of 'institution' is 'an organisation founded for a purpose'. There can be no doubt that a multitude of institutions have nurtured, supported and promoted Christianity with great effect. It seems likely that God will continue to use institutions and it is a fact that there are people who prefer a highly organised and structured expression of church to something that is informal. That is why there is no paradigm change here. What there is, however, is the emergence of expressions of church spread along a broader bandwidth than previously, a wide spectrum of organisational models which ranges from the most complex and highly systematised denomination to two people meeting over coffee. What the evidence indicates is not a transformation, but a rebalancing or reshaping, as the institutional end of the continuum diminishes and the informal expands.

In the *Investigating the invisible church* study, 40 per cent of respondents indicated that their local churches were too formal. Just 11 per cent said that they had found their congregation too informal. For some the choice not to engage with a local congregation reflects this personal preference. However, for many, their disillusionment stems not from whether the congregation is more or less informal. Rather, it is rooted in what they perceive as the inward-orientated culture which develops when institutions begin to prioritise self-preservation over their core purpose for being. As one young woman articulated, 'Surely churches exist to promote the gospel and Christianity, but it seems to me like they sometimes fossilise it instead.'

Within every denomination there are congregations which thrive. They seem to buck all trends and contradict every stereotype. However, having worked with many such exceptional churches, I am left with the sense that they tend to flourish *despite* their institutional context and heritage, rather than *because* of these. They find institutional space in which to prosper, developing ways of working within an institutional framework, while avoiding it becoming a straitjacket. They do not allow institutionalism to squeeze them into a mould but find a way of living in the Spirit, find ways of benefiting from the positives of being an institution, while avoiding the negatives. They often hold loosely to the tradition they have inherited and feel free to search for riches in other traditions.

For many prospective church-leavers, the phase of 'Asking questions and exploring doubts' on 'The road to post-congregational faith' proposed in Chapter 4, includes questioning the reasons for much of what is involved in congregational life and finding no theological rationale for it. A typical voicing of this came from a middle-aged man who, after nearly twenty years of congregational involvement, reported:

I used to look around me on a Sunday morning and think 'What are we doing? Why are we doing this?' Religion, faith, was important to me – it still is – but it seemed more real in the rest of life than in this strange thing that happened on Sunday mornings . . . I would sometimes think, 'Hey, I'm an intelligent bloke, but I have no idea what's going on here.' After a while, although I tried to fight it off, I found myself becoming critical. Not of people so much, but the words of songs, the churchy jargon, the Christian catchphrases. It all just niggled and began to eat away at me. Even the kids noticed that I was not – well, not at my best – when we came home from church. I didn't like the person I was becoming.

The picture is consistent across the Western world: the Church's mode of being is shifting rapidly from being predominantly institutional towards patterns of fellowship and discipleship that are characterised by small, loosely organised, relational groups. Based on his extensive research in the USA, George Barna predicts that, although, in the year 2000, 70 per cent of Christians saw the local church congregation as their primary means of spiritual experience and expression, this will drop to 30–35 per cent by 2025. This corresponds to a parallel rise in what he termed 'alternative faith-based community'. In 2000 he found that just 5 per cent of Christians in the USA viewed these informal expressions as their main context of fellowship and worship, but, based on his data, predicted this proportion to rise to 30–35 per cent by 2025.

This parallels trends in wider society for organisations, commercial and social, to move towards more open cultures and flatter, less hierarchical structures. In making this observation, there is no suggestion that churches are consciously mimicking organisations in other spheres of life. Nor is it implied that they are succumbing to the shifting cultural tides or the latest whims of business, education or any other sector. The point being made is that this is a change of such breadth and depth that it transcends personal preferences; there is a sense of a change in the zeitgeist of the Christian community across the Western world, a shift in the cultural climate.

Changing challenges and challenging changes?

In a few cases, businesses and third-sector organisations have succeeded in negotiating the challenging transition from traditional bureaucracy to more organic and flexible ways of working. However, these are the exceptions. In general, the trend away from 'mechanistic' structures and towards the 'organic', predicted by gurus of organisational theory back in the 1950s, has occurred through the demise of the former and the flourishing of new initiatives that exemplify the latter. The almost playful culture of a global giant like Google, epitomised in their adage 'You can be serious without a suit', has come to symbolise an organisation that is well-adapted to both its context and its purpose.

Within the Christian community too there are examples of large congregations within historical denominations, which have re-imagined church and made courageous decisions to deconstruct their institutional framework in order to implement their vision of a simpler way of being church. However, this is rare – and hugely challenging. While living in Nepal I came across a proverb which translates as 'You can put a dog's tail in a pipe for seven years, but it will still come out bent'! I guess it is the Nepali equivalent of the proverbial leopard's spots. When churches are rooted in denominations that have developed over centuries rather than decades, transition to something significantly different from that which they have inherited is beyond the capacity of most congregations. The big picture is of decline of the institutional and growth in the organic.

Three roots of sorrow

In itself this shift in the balance within the Christian family should be a source of relief and hope: relief because the haemorrhaging of church-goers does not equate to the corresponding decline of Christianity that has sometimes been portrayed; hope because Christian fellowship is being manifested in fresh ways. However, while it may evoke these positive perspectives, the same changes are also the origin of at least three interrelated sources of pain.

First, for the multitudes of people who have a strong emotional attachment to particular institutions that are now in serious decline and for those whose natural inclinations make institutional religion attractive, stimulating and helpful, the 'falling away' of many people and the resultant pressure that mount for those who remain is a source of grief. For some this is aggravated by a sense of guilt, a feeling that long-established churches have gone into a tailspin 'on their watch'.

In view of this first source of pain, there is an urgent need for leaders within the institutional church to recognise the wider picture, to articulate this within congregations and to give serious pastoral attention where people are struggling with the sorrow as they mourn dying congregations. Denial or unrealistic optimism only exacerbates the situation. I remember a rousing address at the annual gathering of a denomination that is in steeper decline than most. The speaker gave a stirring upbeat statement in which he exclaimed, 'We are not managing decline; we are planning for growth'. It is good to plan for growth, but there is also a crying need for the wise and compassionate management of decline.

A second source of pain comes from the possessiveness of some congregations. As has been explored and illustrated in previous chapters, a typical journey out of congregational life is characterised by a long period of soul-searching, frustration and disappointment. For this to be intensified by any implications of disloyalty to God or to the congregation is, in most cases, inappropriate and unnecessarily harrowing for church-leaver and congregation alike. One person who left church after twenty years of intensive involvement entered into correspondence with me after hearing about my research and told me about the encouragement he experienced when visiting a parish church to take a family member to an event there. In the entrance of the building was a prominent banner with the following wording:

Welcome to [name of congregation]. We recognise an important distinction between religious needs and spiritual needs. We believe that everyone has spiritual needs – searchings, longings, questions about what it is to be human and what life is all about – but that not everyone seeks to answer these in a religious way, or by belonging to a church. However they are expressed, we consider these deep spiritual needs to be valid and important in their own right, and we believe it is central to our role, as a community-based church, to help people to voice their questions about life and its meaning and to help seek answers to them, whether these answers take a 'religious' form or not. If their search leads people into the congregation, they will find a welcome, but our concern for them and openness to them is unconditional.

When a congregation, as communicated in the wording of this banner, sees itself not as the sole legitimate context for Christian journeying, but as a resource to both those who stay and those

who pass through, pain associated with different ideas about loyalty and commitment will be prevented. As discussed in Chapter
2, the term 'spiritual butterflies' is used to refer to the phenomenon of people moving from one source of fellowship to another.
It is usually used in a derogatory sense, implying that sustenance
is received, but nothing offered in return. Alan Jamieson, drawing
a parallel between the migration of butterflies and the transitions
of the Christian life, points out the essential role of 'waystations'
if butterflies are to survive the journey. The research among
church-leavers shows that, for some Christians, disenchantment
with church and wrestling with faith-related issues is integral, perhaps essential, to their growth. As interviews with such people
reveal, phases of this kind of grappling and disillusionment can
be protracted experiences of isolation, anguish and confusion.
Congregations and other Christian communities that understand
Paul's instruction to 'help others with encouraging words' and
not to 'drag them down by finding fault'[12] as applying beyond the
circle of those who are able to offer any ongoing contribution,
will provide valuable support for weary travellers and foster a
healthy culture for all who choose to stay.

A third source of pain associated with the reconfiguring of the
Christian community to being less institutional and more organic
and informal is created when people who belong to different
expressions of church fail to recognise each other as authentic
parts of the Christian family. The new can be dismissed as the
latest breakaway, schism or faction; the old can be written off
as outmoded, out-of-touch and irrelevant. The writer Lucy Berry
has a perceptive and provocative poem in her book *Trouble with
church?* in which she imagines a family gathered around the hospital bed of the dying church. She evokes an emotive blend of reverence, sorrow and denial that captures well the position in which
some Christians find themselves. There is a powerful emotional
attachment to the way faith had been expressed and practised
in the past and a deep sadness that what has been a source of
blessing to them is passing – and that others fail to recognise or

---

12. Romans 14:19 (MSG).

value its contribution. However, in a particularly powerful, even prophetic, final paragraph we discover that, just down the same hospital corridor, accompanied by the usual agony and bawling, a new church is being born! After the melancholy scene of grief and angst in one room, the reader now has cause for encouragement. Yes, there is decay and death, but there is also new life. This is good news indeed. But, as is often the case when one hears the words of a prophet, we are left feeling deeply challenged and distinctly uncomfortable. In a final aside, we are informed that the newborn bares so little family resemblance as to be unrecognisable to the family!

Rewilding the Church

Rewilding is a concept that has become important in the field of ecology over the past couple of decades. It proposes a radical new approach to conservation. Instead of preserving landscapes and ecosystems by managing and controlling and protecting, it is suggested that nature should be allowed to follow its own course. While traditional conservation looks for inspiration to the past and seeks to preserve or restore, rewilding looks to the future by resisting the temptation to intervene. Rather than seeing the natural environment as a landscape and a collection of species, it focuses on the constantly developing relationships between all aspects of the ecosystem. A prominent proponent of rewilding likens conventional approaches to conservation to keeping nature in a state of suspended development as if it were a 'jar of pickles'.

You may feel that I'm rather straying from the point here! However, there are parallels between the notion of rewilding and ideas that have developed on both sides of the Atlantic which champion an approach to church variously described as 'liquid church',[13] 'organic church'[14] or, more prevalent in the

---

13. Ward, P., 2001, *Liquid church*, Peabody, MA: Hendrickson.
14. Cole, N., 2005, *Organic church*, San Francisco, CA: Jossey-Bass.

UK, 'missional communities'[15] and 'simple church'.[16] Beneath the diversity of terminology lies a common commitment to gathering as Christians in ways that reflect the historical marks of church, but which resist all but essential structures or procedures in order to ensure that resources are not diverted from core matters of fellowship, mission, worship and discipleship.

More importantly, there are similarities between the underlying philosophy of rewilding, the growing chorus of voices advocating a radical simplifying of church and also what is actually happening. I'm not suggesting that the multitudes of people who have joined the ranks of churchless faith in recent years are consciously involved in a rewilding of the Church. However, as we observe the changes that have occurred, this is what has happened. In recent history at least, people have tended to understand church in terms of certain activities, roles and ways of doing things, but where post-congregational church is emerging it is shaped by the people, their gifts, visions and relationships. Churches that are emerging through the movements explored in this book tend to view growth as something that happens by multiplication rather than addition. Whereas traditional churches have often come to understand mission in terms of activities and events, there is a trend towards an emphasis on being missional in everyday life – from doing mission to being involved in God's mission.

Seeds of hope

We live in an era of great challenge and rare opportunity for Christian communities across the Western world. In Europe especially, it is many centuries since the Christian faith had less prominence in society and less allegiance than it has at present. Since beyond living memory, the primary way of communicating the faith has been through intergenerational transference between

---

15. McNeal, R., 2011, *Missional communities: The rise of the post-congregational church*, San Francisco, CA: Jossey-Bass.

16. Dale, T. and Dale, F., 2002, *Simply church*, Manchaca, TX: Karis.

parents and children reinforced by the faithful labours of Sunday School teachers. Congregations are in decline because people are leaving for reasons explored in the preceding chapters, but mainly because more and more people never engage with congregations in the first place. The 2015 *Faith in Scotland* study found a stark contrast between generations in their attitudes to faith. Among those born before 1945, 68 per cent reported that their faith was important to them. This declined with each subsequent generation, with only 16 per cent of those born since 1981 indicating that their faith was of importance to them. Nearly half (48 per cent) of Anglican churches report fewer than five children (under the age of 16) in their congregations.[17] Based on church attendance or affiliation, it would be correct to conclude that each generation is less religious than the last across the Western world.

However, at the very same time as religious institutions struggle to maintain viability, there is a hunger for meaning and spirituality. Church-leavers have often been dismissed as 'backsliders' and those identifying themselves as 'spiritual but not religious' (SBNR) are distained as 'fuzzy fence-sitters',[18] 'self-indulgent, narcissistic individualists'[19] or worse. However, the evidence reveals a different picture. A growing body of findings challenges the stereotype of individualistic iconoclasts. Studies in the USA indicate that the SBNR phenomenon is growing faster and has greater substance and depth than previously assumed. Although characterised by a dislike of 'the institutional', it is far from being

---

17. Church of England Church Growth Research Programme, 2014, *From anecdote to evidence: Findings of the Church Growth Research Programme 2011–2013*, London: Church of England Archbishops' Council, p. 23.

18. Aune, K., 2014, July 31, review of *Belief without borders: Inside the minds of the spiritual but not religious* by Linda A. Mercadante. Retrieved from www.timeshighereducation.co.uk/books/belief-without-borders-inside-the-minds-of-the-spiritual-but-not-religious-by-linda-a-mercadante/2014785.article.

19. Daniel, L., 2013, *When "spiritual but not religious" is not enough: Seeing God in surprising places, even the church*, Nashville, TN: Jericho Books.

the preserve of isolated individualists; there is a plethora of gatherings, groups and 'considerable theological depth' according to the 2014 research of a professor of historical theology at the Methodist Theological School in Ohio.[20]

The scale of the SBNR phenomenon is undisputable: a survey conducted by the Pew Research Center in 2012 found that 37 per cent of those who identified themselves as unaffiliated to any religious denomination (a group which increased from just over 15 per cent to just under 20 per cent of all US adults in the previous five years) identified themselves as SBNR.[21]

In the preceding chapters you have heard the voices of some church-leavers and other Christians who have no history of church-going who have become the pioneers of alternative expressions of Christian community. Some have done so intentionally, others unwittingly. Often embryonic and frequently unconventional, the ancient and the innovative are often intertwined. Mustard seeds of faith are germinating, offering reminders of the fundamental Christian calling to 'follow me' and, perhaps, giving glimpses of the shape of things to come. At the same time many historical denominations endeavour to shed risk-averse cultures, rediscover the simple essence of Christian community and encourage a wave of missional entrepreneurism. The Church of Scotland's *Church without walls* report challenged the congregations to 'turn again to be people with Jesus at the centre, travelling wherever Jesus takes us'.[22] Such an exhortation, captivating in its simplicity and rousing in its immense implications, eclipses all considerations of denomination or church government. Such things seem paltry in comparison to the high calling to be disciples of Christ.

---

20. Mercadante, L. A., 2014, *Belief without borders: Inside the minds of the spiritual but not religious*, New York: Oxford University Press.

21. Pew Research Center, 2012, October 9, *"Nones" on the rise: One-in-five adults have no religious affiliation*. Retrieved from www.pewforum.org/2012/10/09/nones-on-the-rise/ p. 45–47.

22. The Special Commission anent Review and Reform, 2001, *A church without walls*, Edinburgh: The General Assembly of the Church of Scotland. p. 8.

In one sense, it is sad that, at a time when many denominations are discovering an appetite for planting new expressions of church, many of the pioneers have left. Fortunately, however, at least some of these pioneers are undeterred by their lack of institutional affiliations. There is a growing realisation that church is what occurs when people are touched by the living Christ and share the journey of faith with others. Whether that occurs in an historic building or online or . . . wherever, is unimportant.

So what?
Questions and activities for further reflection

We began this book with the words of Jesus: 'Take a good look at what is right in front of you.' Who could you draw together to discuss how the issues raised by this book are reflected in your local area?

Is there a burning question provoked by reading this book, but left unanswered? Write it down and commit to finding answers.

Is there a personal challenge that has taken hold of you during your reading? Resolve to follow a course of action and pray for God's help in that.

Has something resonated with you that you might investigate further? Revisit the references and consider whether some further reading might help as you continue your own journey.

While finishing this final chapter the most recent contribution to our knowledge of churchless faith rolled off the press in the USA. Sociologists Josh Packard and Ashleigh Hope entitle their book: *Church refugees: Sociologists reveal why people are done with church but not their faith*.[23] (I feel like shouting 'Snap'!) One definition of 'refugee' is a person who has fled from some danger or problem. It comes from a French word meaning 'gone in search of refuge'. Having heard the evidence, make a list of 'dangers or problems' that churchless Christians seek freedom from – and the ways they are finding refuge.

---

23. Packard, J. and Hope, A., 2015, *Church refugees: Sociologists reveal why people are done with church but not their faith*, Loveland, CO: Group Publishing.

Bible References Index

Name and Subject Index